Super Saints Book II

Holy Innocence

The Young and the Saintly

Bob and Penny Lord

Journeys of Faith®
1-800-633-2484

Books by Bob and Penny Lord

This Is My Body, This Is My Blood
Miracles of the Eucharist - Book I

This Is My Body, This Is My Blood
Miracles of the Eucharist - Book II
The Many Faces of Mary, a Love Story
We Came Back to Jesus
Saints and Other Powerful Women in the Church
Saints and Other Powerful Men in the Church
Heavenly Army of Angels
Scandal of the Cross and Its Triumph
Martyrs - They Died for Christ
The Rosary - the Life of Jesus and Mary
Visionaries, Mystics and Stigmatists
Visions of Heaven, Hell and Purgatory
Trilogy Book I - Treasures of the Church
Trilogy Book II - Tragedy of the Reformation
Trilogy Book III - Cults: Battle of the Angels
Super Saints Book I - Journey to Sainthood
Super Saints Book II - Holy Innocence
Super Saints Book III - Defenders of the Faith
Este es Mi Cuerpo, Esta es Mi Sangre
Milagros de la Eucaristía
Los Muchos Rostros de Maria una historia de amor

ISBN 1-58002-133-6

Holy Innocence

Table of Contents

Dedication

We love our children and our young people very much. They are the future; they are the present; they are the hope of the Church, of the world. We believe our young are in a crisis, with the world crashing down on them. Everyone is vying for their souls. The enemy is doing everything to win them over to hell. We have a need and a sincere desire to reach out, and touch them, and tell them the Lord loves them; the Lord needs them.

In this book, we are trying to bring the youth of today - Role Models who will lead them to God, touchable Saints, young and vulnerable like them, who struggled with the crises of their times and fought; and having fought - won the war for Jesus, for the Church, for their immortal souls. We have come to realize that we're not alone by any means. There are people out there who care and are trying with all their might to win over the young of our world for Jesus:

Pope John Paul II - It is exciting to be at a Congress for Youth and see their reaction to *their* Pope, as they chant in many languages, over and over again, *"Juan Pablo Segundo, te quiere todo el mundo!"* (John Paul the Second, the whole world loves you!) They love him, and he loves them! Here is a man in his seventies, advocating holiness and values, foreign to the philosophy of the world, and the young are responding! An army is forming behind the Vicar of Christ! He has called the young to take their rightful role in the world. Pope John Paul considers the youth a culture of its own, the Church of today and tomorrow.

Mother Mary Angelica, and her Poor Clare Nuns of Perpetual Adoration - They are an ongoing sign to us that striving for holiness, living a virtuous, pious life is not something untouchable, not dead bones which cannot be revived; it is alive and well, and growing in Birmingham, Alabama in a Poor Clare Convent of cloistered Nuns faithfully living out their Rule. In a time when we are told there is a crisis in vocations, Mother Angelica cannnot accomodate all who wish to enter her community. In a world where we are told to do our own thing, we are free, individual, only live once, being fed pablum which tells us it is impossible in our society to be obedient and chaste, we find an oasis in the desert where beautiful flowers are blooming, Brides of Christ whose lanterns are filled with oil, awaiting the *Bridegroom*.

Fr Giovanni Alberti, C.P. of the Sanctuary of Maria Goretti, Nettuno Italy - Fr. Alberti took time out on the day they were setting up for the feast of St. Maria Goretti in Nettuno, to give us the background of the shrine, and his own insights into the life of this most famous saint. *We would also like to thank the priests and lay people in Corinaldo, Italy,* for giving us invaluable material and allowing us to videotape for EWTN, the life of Maria Goretti, bringing us to the house where she lived and was martyred to preserve her chastity.

The Passionist Fathers and brothers, Custodians of the Shrine of St. Gabriel Possenti in Isola di Gran Sasso, Italy - Eager to reach young people who wish to learn about their Saint, they gave us great insights and information, for our book, and video, on St. Gabriel, a challenging touchable Saint for all time,

Salesian custodians at Don Bosco's Oratory in Turin, Italy, and the priests and brothers at Colle Don Bosco, near his birthplace in Becchi, Italy - Dominic Savio was an extremely important part of Don Bosco's work with children. The Salesians who have continued with his work with young people gave us much cooperation in tracking the life of Dominic Savio with regards to Don Bosco, and also his home in Chieri, Italy.

The Custodian of the Shrine of St. Philomena in Mugnano del Cardinale, Italy - Truly a Saint of the youth, who gave her life to preserve her chastity and virginity. This tribute to her, near Avellino, Italy, is a haven for young people, as the priests and sisters there reach out to the young with a powerful Virgin and Martyr, a Role Model for these final days.

And lastly, thank you, *Rob and Andrea Ziminsky,* for giving us hope for the future of the Church and the world.

Where have all the Children Gone?

We have just returned from Italy, where we spent three weeks videotaping shrines of the Saints who form this book and television Series for EWTN of the same name. In addition, we led a group of pilgrims from all over the United States to the Shrines of Italy. It was beautiful as it always is, but there was something missing, which was just an undercurrent at the beginning of our journey, but by the end, rang loud and clear in our hearts. *There were no children!!*

We traveled to Sorrento and Capri, which are not typical religious shrines; they are more secular, devoted to the beach and summer fun. Our focus was the background of a Saint who is loved and respected in that area, St. Anthony Abate, the hermit. In addition, we videotaped the artwork in the Cathedral that we remembered from when we used to come to this beautiful town in the late '70's with our grandson, and he celebrated Mass as Altar Boy in that church. Normally, children would be all over Sorrento, especially in the summer. There were great crowds, more teenagers and young adults than we'd like to think of, and senior citizens galore, but very few children.

Italians love their children. They spoil them excessively. They dress them like little lords and ladies. It had always been a treat for us to go over to Italy and just take in how the parents would dawdle over their children, and how the children could get anything they wanted by pressing a few emotional buttons or pulling a few heartstrings of the adults. We marveled at how families thrived, despite the Italians voting overwhelmingly for Abortion in the late '70's or early '80's. We recalled how Pope John Paul II, a new Pope at the time, pleaded with the Italian people not to vote for abortion in this special referendum they held. It was to no avail. Abortion was in. But it didn't seem to have any effect on the Italians, not until now.

We asked the priests at various shrines we visited, what was happening in Italy. Some shrugged their shoulders. Others told us it's not just Italy; it's the whole world. But Italy is very pronounced because of the great number of Senior citizens. Others would blame the satan of Planned Parenthood and Abortion. Said the head of one shrine, "No one wants the inconvenience or sacrifice connected with big families today. In addition, many parents feel they can't afford children or more children. Others say they want to wait until they've finished climbing the corporate ladder before they burden themselves down with a family." There is absolutely no balance whatsoever.

Only on the last day in Assisi did we see a number of young parents with their babies and strollers, promenading through the medieval city of St. Francis. They were beautiful and the parents had them dressed as little dolls. This was the Italy we had been used to seeing. But there were only a handful of them, and they were the exception rather than the rule.

When we returned to the United States this week, we tried to go through some issues of the Wanderer which we may have missed. What do you think we saw on the first page of one of the issues? "New York Times - Finally - Recognizes the Demographic Death of Europe." The article tells how the New York Times, which it calls the United States' leading mouthpiece for the 'culture of death' finally acknowledged what most demographers have been saying for over ten years, "Europe is demongraphically dead."

What they're saying in simple terms is that there are more people dying in Europe each year than are being born. We refer to it as a minus zero population growth. We've been talking about it for many years, but this is the first time that a major American newspaper, strongly supportive of birth control, abortion and euthanasia has formally stated that we have a problem in Europe. They state as an example, Bologna, Italy, a university town much like Padua, only bigger. It is a great Italian metropolis. Statistically, women gave birth to less than one baby per person. The figure was 0.8 for 1997. If it continues at this rate, and there is no reason to believe it won't, in twenty years, for every child under the age of five, there will be 25 over the age of 50, and 10 of those will be older than 80.

The same situation applies in other European cities, including Germany, Greece and Spain, where there are more people over age 60 than under age 20. Compare that with **Iraq**, where **half** the population is *under 25*, or **Palestine**, where the average woman gives birth to **8.8** children, as opposed to Italy's 0.8. Although there were no statistics given for the United States, our situation is not much better. We read recently that in the United States, we have about 1.3 children per family. That's not anywhere near Palestine's 8.8 per family. We recall during the Persian Gulf crisis, when we lived in Southern California, our cable television company carried a channel which was Arabic. A caucasian woman dressed as an Arab got on television and said she wished the Arabs would not take part in armed conflict with Americans. "We will take you over by sheer numbers!" she stated, meaning the propulation explosion which the Arabs are promolgating, as opposed to the negative population growth of most other ethnic groups, including Americans.

Where have all the Children gone? Where are the Sts. Dominic Savios, Gabriel of the Sorrows, Maria Gorettis, Aloysius Gonzagas, Stanislaus Kostkas, Margaret of Castellos, Philomenas, Rose of Viterbos of this age or the age to come? Where are the role models for the young people? Our dear Pope has realized the importance of youth not only in the Church, but in the world. He considers youth to be a society and culture of its own. How can we propogate and nurture this culture if it doesn't exist? How can we draw on the next generation to run our countries and our world if they have not been born, if they will never be born?

In the Wanderer article taken from the New York Times, in an attempt to root out the cause of the problem, it ends with a statement made by a thirty-one year old Swedish biologist: "We have become so selfish, so greedy. Did our parents sit down with a spread sheet and figure out whether they could afford to have two or three children? No, of course not. Did this ever happen before anywhere? No, of course not! We live in the richest place and at the best time, and everyone is worrying whether they can afford to take their next vacationor buy a boat. It's kind of sickening, really."

Sickening yes, but more than that, deadly. Where have all the children gone? They must be brought back. If we want to save the world and the Church, we must bring young people to the Lord. The greatest attack in the Twentieth Century has been on the family. If the enemy is to be successful in destroying family, the priesthood and ultimately the Church, all he has to do is stop the flow of Catholics coming into the world. Who can bring the children back to the Church and to the world? Only you, my brothers and sisters, only you.

*St. Gabriel Possenti
Patron of Youth*

Above: *St. Gabriel's mother wanted to
embrace him before she died.*

Above: *Shrine of St. Gabriel Possenti in
Teramo, Italy*

Above: *Profession of
St. Gabriel as a Passionist*

St. Gabriel Possenti

Co- Patron of Italian Catholic Youth

St. Gabriel Possenti was twenty-four years old when he died. We are always asked the question, *"Why does God take someone in the prime of their life and snuff out that life?"* We don't really know the answer, but we can muse; we can speculate; we can try to understand what God's plan for a particular person at a particular time might be. Or we might try to determine how the life of that person can change the world of his time or ours.

Francesco Possenti was such a person! He was given to us to do great things for the Lord; not only in life but in death. He made such an impact on the people of his time that he became known as a *Saint of the Youth*. He was born in Assisi on March 1, 1838. What was going on in Assisi and Italy in 1838 which would cause the Lord to bring a special child into the world, who would glorify His Name in twenty-four short years, much like our Little Flower, St. Thérèse of Lisieux? Why did the Lord choose Assisi as his birthplace, that famous city graced by the presence of God's other special son, St. Francis?

Europe had become extremely anti-clerical during that time. Remember, it was in 1830 that Our Lady appeared to St. Catherine Labourè in Paris and told her about the suffering the Church would have to endure. In 1846, our Lady appeared to two children in La Salette, France, and wept the entire time, grieving because the people were behaving so contemptuously towards her Son. But She assigned the task of righting wrongs to two little children. When she was preparing to leave the children, she said to them, *"But you will make my words known to all the people."*[1] The Church, the world is in trouble, Our Lady reaches out to another young person to help Her mend the wounds inflicted on Her Son's Church and the children who

---

[1] Read more about these Apparitions of Mother Mary in Bob and Penny Lord's book: *"The Many Faces of Mary, a love story"*

11

belong to her. St. Gabriel Possenti, whose religious name was Brother Gabriel of the Sorrowful Virgin, was one of those whom She chose.

Our Lady wept in 1846 because she knew the state of Mother Church, the critical aftermath of having been weakened by the imprisonment of Pope Pius VII for five years by Napoleon Bonaparte (from 1809 to 1814). It was more than the physical disgrace our Pope had to endure. Napoleon crippled the Church, making her into a second-class power. He did this with complete disdain for the great history and rich traditions from which she emanated and for Jesus, Who instituted the Church at the Last Supper. Napoleon reduced Italy to a mere possession of the French Empire. He closed down all religious institutions, such as the Franciscan community in Assisi. The upper Basilica of St. Francis was used as a stable for the horses of Napoleon's troops. This was a period of abject contempt for Mother Church from which it would take her years to come out from under. In 1815, Napoleon was defeated and the Pope was restored to power; but the Church was still very weak and disrespected by all the powers of Europe. Many of the kings and princes of Europe enjoyed the ill treatment our Pope and the Church had received at the hands of Napoleon Bonaparte.

It took military intervention for the Popes to maintain control over the papal lands, and which country was willing to aid the Papacy was based on who was at war with whom at any given time. Little principalities wanted to take away the papal lands and the Pope's power. The situation had pretty well deteriorated from the time of Napoleon. By 1831, after a revolution in Bologna, which spread its poison to the provinces of Romagna, the Marches (Ancona) and the Umbria (Assisi), the only way the Pope was able to get back into power and maintain any semblance of respect for the Papacy, was through bargaining with the Austrians and the French. These two powers intervened in the fracas by supplying the Pope military support.

At about the time Francesco Possenti was born, the Pope

was under tremendous pressure from political groups from without, and reform groups from within, trying to pattern the country after Napoleon Bonaparte's method of governing. One thing they would not do is equate the papal monarchy with the Church itself. The Papal authority had always been based on Divine Right.[2] Criticism of the Pope or the Papacy was considered irreverence towards God Himself. Revolutionary attempts against the papal monarchy and the papal states were considered sacrilegious. This is how the papacy was conceived prior to the abuses of the Renaissance, the division caused by the Protestant Reformation, the free-thinking of the Age of Reason and the Age of Enlightenment, the chaotic French Revolution, Napoleon Bonaparte, and this last attack, just prior to Garibaldi's unification of Italy.

The powers of Europe had lived with this understanding of their relationship with the Church for centuries. It was not until the Church lost the respect of the monarchs of different nations, which began with the Renaissance, escalated through the alliance of Martin Luther and the German princes, was then compounded by a former ally Henry VIII, devastated by a bloodthirsty maniac - John Calvin, and just about brought to her knees by Napoleon Bonaparte, a common soldier who went out of his way to desecrate the Church and all it held dear, that the rulers of Europe saw a way of breaking the power of the Papacy for good. They tried to impose sanctions and mandates on the Pope which were nothing short of degrading and contemptuous. Remember, we're talking here of a Secular Ruler as well as a Spiritual Ruler. It seemed outrageous to think that a papal monarch would share power or be subservient in any way to secular powers or leaders. The powers that be, wanted to separate the role of land baron and Pastor of the flock.

When Pope Pius IX assumed the pontificate of the

---

[2]explained fully in Bob and Penny Lord's book, *Treasures of the Church, that which makes us Catholic, Book I* on the Trilogy of the Church

Catholic world, he tried to put a stop to, or at least halt the acceleration of the overthrow of the papal lands. But whatever he was able to do was not enough to stem the momentum which had begun centuries before. The people of the regions had been so beaten down by rebel forces, that when it came time to take a vote, whether they wanted to remain papal states, or join the new United Italy, they overwhelmingly voted to join the new State. To be fair, it was either that or suffer dire consequences. A bishop was murdered in Rome; the Pope had to retreat from the city; the revolutionaries came in and declared Rome the capital of the new Kingdom of Italy.

All of this took place during the lifetime of Francesco Possenti, the last of which occurred the year before he died, in 1861. Because of a vow made by Napoleon III[3] to defend the papal states by force, if necessary, it took another ten years before the Vatican was successfully seized. In 1870, because the French were losing bitterly in the Franco-Prussian War, Napoleon III had to withdraw his troops and support, and the cannons were free to attack the Vatican; the Pope became formally, a *hostage* in the Vatican. The final death knell was sounded for the papal states in 1929 when Benito Mussolini forced the Pope into signing the *Lateran Pacts Treaty*, which eliminated any papal property left and created the tiny country called the State of Vatican City.

✞ ✞ ✞

A Gentle Breeze From Heaven

You can see how in need the people of God were for the Father to come to them in some form and affirm that He was still with them, working powerfully in their behalf. To this end, He gave the gift of a son to Sante Possenti and Agnese Frisciotti.[4] Sante was the governor of Assisi at the time (1838), and therefore involved in all the political intrigues which were

---

[3]Napoleon III, nephew of Napoleon Bonaparte, was an ally of the Pope.
[4]Women in Italy did not give up their maiden name when they married.

prevailing in the Church and the State. The child was named Francesco, in honor of the other Francis who made that town famous, St. Francis of Assisi. The home was filled with the joy of God until 1842, when Francesco was four years old. His dear mother was taken from him in death. Francesco was devastated. He didn't understand death at the time - why his mother had to die and couldn't be with him any more. His older sister, Maria Louise, vowed to care for Francesco, who was the eleventh of a family of thirteen, and therefore still very young. She helped her father rear her siblings for as long as she could. Cholera robbed Francesco of his *second mother*, when he was barely seventeen years old.

Although he was growing into a young man, the death of his sister broke his heart. If it was possible, he was more deeply moved by this loss than by the loss of his mother. It was very possible that the reason for this was because he was so young when his mother died; even though he had been very close to her, he did not live as much of his life with her as he had with this sister. Maria Louise's death was very traumatic for the young boy. By this time, 1855, they had moved to Spoleto, which is about forty miles from Assisi, actually a much bigger town than Assisi. The father's new position as registrar of the town, was very prestigious, but very time consuming. He found himself heavily involved in the politics of the municipality, and therefore did not have much time for Francesco. So the loss of the sister had a greater impact on him. She had always been there for him. She was his best friend, his confidante. He could share all his dreams, his love of Our Lord Jesus and Our dear Mother Mary, the Angels and the Saints. He could go to the local church, and spend time there with the Lord. Marie Louise would always cover for him if he came home late, or did not get his chores done on time.

Her death did not depress him, however, which would have been natural, especially for a young man of his age, and since they had been so close. No, what he got from her death

Left: *St. Gabriel found a broken statue of Our Lady.*
He cleaned it, repaired it, and painted it with loving kindness.

Right:
St. Gabriel attended Mass inside the cloister area in this chapel.

Left:
St. Gabriel's original room inside the cloister area in the Passionist Monastery in Teramo, Italy

was a deep awareness of the frailty of life, how our lives on earth were merely a pilgrimage to Heaven, man's true journey on earth. Life was too short to waste on frivolous things. It just didn't make sense to Francesco. He immersed himself in the beauty of the Church, and matters of the Kingdom. He wanted to spend all his time around Jesus, with Jesus, learning about Jesus.

And this, my brothers and sisters, is where Jesus provides us with the great contradiction. Here, the paradox comes in. And it is just this. At a time when the Church had lost its popularity, when the majesty and reverence was being taken away, when everything exalted about our Faith was being ripped from their hearts, a young man, who had been greatly influenced by the politics of the time, finds himself irresistibly drawn to that Church and his only desire - to submerge himself completely into Jesus.

One of the greatest gifts of St. Gabriel Possenti was his values, his priorities. While others were distancing themselves from Mother Church, and selling their souls for position in government, in nobility, a young man from the inside, from the very core of political life that others were vying for, rejected that life and those values, and embraced Church and all that it held for him. He was a contradiction in terms. He wanted to be completely immersed in Jesus; and yet he loved the world and everything in it.

St. Gabriel Possenti grew up as a regular boy. He was a prankster; he enjoyed parties; loved to dance, was extremely good-looking and possibly a little vain. He was the life of the party, very popular. He was called the "Dancer." He loved the girls and had no desire to give up any of it. As a matter of fact, his father had tried to match him up with a local girl, Maria Pannechetti. But although they were close friends, they had never considered marrying each other.

But with all of his fun-loving ways, there was something missing. There was a gnawing at his heart which he could not explain, and could not satisfy. He adored Church and all things that had to do with the Catholic Faith. But that was just who he was. That didn't mean he wanted to give up his life to Jesus and Mary in a Religious community. He constantly vacillated, *"should I, shouldn't I?"* Although everyone could see his virtues, they couldn't take him seriously. He was what we call a Beau Brummel. He had to have the latest fashions. His grooming was of the utmost importance to him. He had to be just so. The social life of Spoleto beckoned him and he gladly embraced it.

But then on the other side of the coin, he showed a great desire to join the Jesuits, which was not an easy order to enter. His father allowed him to request admission from the Jesuits, knowing full well that if by some strange quirk, they should admit him, Francesco would back out and never enter the order. And Francesco did not disappoint his father. He couldn't pull himself away from the parties and the friends.

The outbreak of cholera in 1855, which took Francesco's sister, had reached epidemic proportions. It was raging out of control, especially in Spoleto. The parties ended because most everyone was either sick from the cholera or had died from the dreaded disease. The Bishop of Spoleto asked the people to join him marching in a procession, petitioning Our Lady using an ancient Byzantine icon of her and the Baby Jesus as their standard-bearer. Francesco (St. Gabriel) joined with the rest of the community, to pray that Our Lord Jesus, through the intercession of Our Lady, would spare the community of Spoleto from losing any more of the faithful, as a result of the cholera. The Bishop promised Our Lord and Our Lady that the people of the Diocese would make an annual procession in her honor if the request was granted.

The Lord responded. The people processed, and the outbreak of cholera in the area of Spoleto was halted; there were no more deaths due to this terrible disease. Everyone was grateful. A year passed; true to their word, the people of the diocese of Spoleto marched again, in procession, only this time it was in thanksgiving. This turned out to be a very special procession for Francesco. It was during this time that the Lord spoke to him. As he knelt before the image of Our Lady, he heard in his heart: *"Francesco, why do you remain in the world? It is not for you. Follow your vocation."*

There are so many similarities between the life of St. Francis of Assisi and his namesake, Francesco Possenti. They both felt the lure of the world. They were both popular among the other youths and leaders of their social circles. They both felt the call of the Lord. They both heard the Lord speak to their hearts and in both instances it was in Spoleto.

Francesco felt the calling to enter religious life as a member of the Passionist community. But he had just graduated from the Jesuit college! As a matter of fact, he was asked to give the graduation ceremony speech. He knew he could not possibly apply for entrance in a religious community without his father's blessings, so he decided to do the natural thing. He began to wear his father down. He asked his father permission to join the Passionist brothers. The father turned him down flat. At first blush, this seems a little contradictory, in that one of his brothers, Aloysius, was a Dominican priest, and the family had thirteen children. However, then we find that of the thirteen, seven had died, not necessarily all from the cholera epidemic. But there were only six left. The father didn't want to lose another child to the Church. In addition, to his way of thinking, Francesco would have been his *last* candidate for religious life. He was not strong enough for the rigor, especially of so strict an order as the Passionists; and quite honestly, his father judged he would not be able to give up the secular world. He loved life too much. The glamour of the world would not let him go, or so the father thought.

Eventually, his father gave in; Francesco received permission to apply to enter the Passionist Order; but the father did everything in his power to prevent his son from going. In addition to trying to distract him with many things of the world, to which the father knew Francesco would fall victim (but he didn't), he actually hid the letter of acceptance Francesco received from the Passionists.

Francesco had waited and waited and (as far as he knew) had never heard anything from them. Finally, he made the decision to go to the Passionist community in Morrovalle, and inquire what happened to his application. He was able to get his brother, the priest, to accompany him for moral support. The father had not given up on Francesco, however. He contacted all the people that the two would visit on their journey to Morrovalle. Now, while it was not that great a distance, they had to go over mountains to arrive at Ancona on the Adriatic Sea and then proceed south to Civitanova Marche and inland to Morrovalle. From Spoleto today, it might take about three hours. At that time, it could have taken a week. And each night, they were staying at friends or relatives whom the father had contacted, to try to dissuade Francesco from joining the Passionists. As it turned out, by the time Francesco and his brother Fr. Aloysius left each home they had visited, they had convinced the friends and relatives that it was the right thing to do, for Francesco to join the Passionist community. The only one who was never convinced was their father, Sante.

The highlight of their trip was their visit to the Holy House of Loreto. They arrived late at night on the octave of her birthday, September 7, which was a particularly crowded period and had to sleep on the floor of a hallway with only mats as their mattresses. While the body suffered greatly this inconvenience, the young future Saint's soul rose to the top of the Basilica in anticipation of being that close to Our Lady in the house where she lived with Jesus and St. Joseph, where the Angel Gabriel appeared to her and told her she was to be the Mother of God. Was it here that Francesco was first given his religious name, Gabriel, in honor of the great Archangel who remained with Mary and Jesus all their lives? Did our Lady speak to his heart here, as he had to Mary's? Could he feel the presence of Gabriel in the Holy House, as he stood beneath the Angel's window?"[5]

The next morning, Francesco's brother Fr. Aloysius was given the honor of celebrating Mass for Our Lady's birthday at the Holy House. Francesco made a general confession to prepare himself to enter the Passionist community in Morrovalle, a short distance from Loreto.

What a surprise Francesco had upon his arrival at the Passionist headquarters in Morrovalle. They had been praying that he would respond to their invitation to join the community, but it had been so long since they had written to him that they were beginning to give up hope. Finally, Francesco and Fr. Aloysius put two and two together and realized that the father had been trying to sabotage Francesco's desire to be a religious. Francesco understood that the entire trip from Spoleto had been one blockade after another put into place by his father to prevent his son from entering the Passionist community. That evening, September 9, Francesco entered and would not leave. Although the official day of his entry into the community was September 10, he was not about to take any chances. He stayed from the minute he arrived. His brother, Fr. Aloysius, and an uncle who had joined them for the last day's journey to the Passionist community, left without him.

The father never backed down. When Francesco took his vows as a brother in the Passionist Order, his father did not come for the ceremony. About two weeks after he entered the community, Francesco wrote his father a letter. It was the Feast of the Sorrowful Virgin, September 21, 1856. In it he said:

"My dearest Father, today, the Feast of Our Lady of the Sorrows, our mother and patron, to my indescribable happiness, I was clothed in the religious habit, taking the name of Confrater Gabriel of the Sorrowful Virgin."

It's not known for sure if Francesco and his father ever

---

[5]For a full explanation of the Holy House of Nazareth in Loreto, Italy, read Bob and Penny Lord's book, *Heavenly Army of Angels*

reconciled, although Francesco wrote to him often. We don't know if they ever saw each other again.

Francesco's new name, *Gabriel of the Sorrowful Virgin*, was one which he cherished for the rest of his life as a religious, which only lasted some five years and a few months. He entered in September 1556; he died in February, 1562. But in this short period of time, a Saint blossomed from out of this young man, a Saint who would be needed for the rough time which was to come for his Church and his country. The Lord demanded of Gabriel all that he could possibly give, and all that he could possibly be, and Gabriel said *yes*.

A transformation took place in those few years from holy person to Saint. It was easier for the Passionist community to accept this change because they witnessed it from its inception to its completion. But for his family and friends, it was very difficult. In 1930, ten years after his canonization, St. Gabriel's brother, Michael Possenti, was interviewed by a Passionist. The question was a natural one. *"Weren't you surprised when you first heard that steps were being taken to have your brother canonized?"*

Michael's answer was a resounding yes! The reason was simple. Although he admitted that Francesco was always a good boy, he was no Saint, while he lived with his family in Spoleto. At least Michael had never seen qualities in his younger brother which would have given him an inkling that he was in the presence of a future Saint. He had never exhibited what Michael would have considered Saintly characteristics.

However, the answer might have been different had the interviewer been able to speak to his deceased sister, Maria Louisa, who was his closest friend and confidante. She may have been able to see the attributes in her younger brother which would one day raise him to the Communion of Saints. She had reached into his soul during his formative years. She had experienced the beginning of her brother's journey toward Sainthood. However, it was a long, arduous road which

Francesco, now Gabriel, would have to travel.

One of the most difficult things for Gabriel to accept and understand was how necessary it was for him *to be*, rather than *to do*. Keep in mind he came from a can-do society. His family gauged its self worth by what it had accomplished, never considering the cost. Brother Gabriel's novice master had to impress upon him that the journey was the dream, his greatest accomplishment would not be in the doing, but in the being. Gabriel worked on humility, which was a difficult virtue for him. This reminds me of a song people used to sing when they were confronted with someone who was just so in love with himself. "Oh Lord, it's hard to be humble, when you're perfect in every way." We believe that Gabriel had to swallow that kind of self-esteem. According to his brother Michael, Francesco was extremely good-looking and knew it. He shared that when they used to go to dances together, the girls would all flock about Francesco and he danced with as many as he could.

He worked on self-denial, not realizing that was a thing to do. He also took on extra tasks, which were also thing-doing. But that's who he was, and that was the path he had to follow to finally achieve the gift of martyrdom to all the things which had been so important to him in his life, not the least of which was giving up things he liked. But it opened him up to the Lord. He had cleaned the house of his spirit so much that he was available to do whatever the Lord would ask of him. He allowed himself to be filled. To quote from a contemporary of his, St. Thérèse of Lisieux, *"And now....something had melted away, and there were no longer two of us - Thérèse had simply disappeared, like a drop lost in the ocean; Jesus only was left, my Master, my King."*[6]

Brother Gabriel had an enormous effect on the other members of the Passionist community at Morrovalle. One of his

---

[6]Read Bob and Penny Lord's *Saints and Other Powerful Women in the Church*

biographers wrote the following of him:

"He was always eager to do more bodily penance, and for a long time, to take a single example, he asked permission to wear a chain set with sharp points. Leave (permission) was refused, but he still begged for it with modest persistence. His director replied, `You want to wear the little chain! I tell you what you really ought to have is a chain on your will - yes, that is what you need. Go away, don't speak to me about it.' And he retired deeply mortified. Another time when he was asking leave for the same thing, `Well, yes,' I said, `wear it by all means; but you must wear it outside your habit and in public, too, that all may see what a man of great mortification you are.' Though stung to the quick, he wore it as I directed; besides, to satisfy his thirst for penance, I made fun of him before his companions; but he accepted all in silence, and did not even ask to be dispensed from thus becoming a laughing stock."[7]

At the end of his novitiate, he and some other young brothers were sent away from Morrovalle south to the province of Abruzzi. They went to a monastery in a small village in the foothills of a mountain called Isola di Gran Sasso. Under normal conditions, they might not have sent these young brothers so far away from the rest of the community, but the situation we described to you at the beginning of the chapter was escalating. The war against the papal states, and the unification of Italy were all manifesting themselves. It was not only not safe for the young Passionists, but it was not a good atmosphere for them to be studying for their vocation, which was the priesthood.

Going to this remote part of Italy was good for Gabriel. He was able to turn off the world, which had been crashing down around him. Rumors abounded about what was happening in the State and in the Church. They were sure that any day they would

---

[7]Butler's Lives of the Saints Vol. 1 - page 430

be attacked by any one of the various political groups who were trying to take over the country. There had been a takeover by the government in Piedmont-Sardegna and church property had been confiscated and secularized. There was fear for the religious communities in the rest of the country as the Unification of Italy became a reality.

Gabriel had always had a great devotion to Our Lady, but this time, these last few years in the mountain town of Isola di Gran Sasso seemed to solidify all that had been between them over the years. It came to bloom when he found a broken statue of Our Lady in a storehouse at the monastery. He cleaned it, repaired it, and painted it, with loving tenderness. By the time he was finished, it was so beautiful, the superior placed it in a special location in the monastery. It was while he was working on this statue, trying to make it the most beautiful image of Our Lady in the whole world, that his love for Her increased. It was as if She were whispering in his ear, sharing gifts about Her life, which he had never known before. He put these insights down in book form and called it *Simbolo Mariano*. There were fifty two points regarding Our Lady.

On September 22, 1857, about a year after he had joined the Passionist community, he made his profession, the ceremony consisted of the Rites of Vestition and Profession. Brother Gabriel and two others were given the badges of the Passionists, black patches embossed with a white cross and heart. In the center of the white heart are the words, Jesu Xpi Passio, the Passion of Christ, with an image of three nails.

As part of the profession ceremony, Fr. Norbert, his novice master, read from John's account of the Passion and Death of Our Lord Jesus. At the words, "He handed over His Spirit," each candidate rose kneeling in front of the altar and made their profession. Gabriel said the following words:

"I, Confrater Gabriel of the Sorrowful Virgin, do vow
and promise by a simple vow and promise, to Almighty
God, to Blessed Mary ever a Virgin, to the whole

*Heavenly court and to you, Father, poverty, chastity and
obedience, as well as a diligent endeavor to promote in
the hearts of the faithful, a lively devotion toward and a
grateful remembrance of, the Passion of Jesus Christ
according to the Rule and Constitution of the Discalced
Clerics of the Cross and Passion of Jesus Christ, until the
end of my life."*

St. Gabriel's father was right about one thing, his physical
stamina. It began to break down not long after he went up to the
monastery on the mountain. As was the case with the Little
Flower, the same occurred to St. Gabriel, although it all
happened before St. Thérèse was even born. While his bodily
strength diminished, his spiritual awareness expanded. It was as
if the Lord had opened an overabundance of spiritual knowledge
which Gabriel shared with his community. Of course, the
superiors were not aware that he was dying, nor was he. So as
he shared the abundant Divine gifts the Lord had accorded him,
all they could think of was what a priest he was going to make,
and how he could use these favors for the Church to whom he
would minister.

Gabriel contracted Tuberculosis. He began to cough up
blood. His health deteriorated quickly. He had to be limited to
the activities he could perform, which didn't make him happy.
However, he was obedient and did what he could, when he was
able. At other times, he spent his days and nights in union with
Our Lord Jesus, His Mother Mary, the Angels and the Saints.
While he was wracked with pain, he was in a form of ecstasy.
And while he had to be taken care of and watched over, those in
whose care he was placed, claimed that he was always joyful and
cheerful. If they hadn't known how sick he was, they would not
have had the slightest inkling from his jocular way.

It was a race against time for our young future Saint. He
continued with his studies, and the preparation of his soul to be a
holy Priest of God, working in the vineyards the Lord would
provide. But his health, and even worse, the political situation,

became his enemy and rival. He studied intensely at Isola di Gran Sasso until May 1861. On May 25, he and his colleagues went to the Cathedral at Penne, which was a mountain trip by foot, where they received the orders of Tonsure and Minor Orders. They were scheduled to return in September to be received in the order of Subdiaconate, and in December the Diaconate, the last step before Ordination to the Priesthood. But the political climate became so bad they had to postpone these ceremonies indefinitely, and as it turned out, until after Gabriel died.

Tuberculosis was a killer of the Nineteenth Century. When the diagnosis was given, it almost certainly meant a death sentence for the poor person who was afflicted with it. Gabriel showed all the signs of a tubercular. His face was pale, emaciated. His chest was sunken, nails arched and pointed. He was thankful that the Lord had graced him with this illness, as it was a lingering disease. He felt sure he could prepare his soul for his entry into the Kingdom.

Attitudes are indicative of where a particular soul resides. Gabriel asked his superior if he could pray for a good and holy death. Fr. Norbert was taken back somewhat by this because the entire community was praying for a total recovery. But he gave Gabriel permission as he had asked. However, he placed a condition on his authorization. He said, "Very well! But first ask for your recovery if it be for God's glory and the salvation of your soul. Otherwise ask God to grant you a happy death."

We believe the Lord gave Gabriel both of his requests. He had a lingering illness, all through the summer and fall of 1861. He died a good and holy death. During his long illness, he was gifted with seeing how very loved he was by his brothers in community. He was given a larger room where he would be more comfortable, but also one which could accommodate the never-ending line of visitors, brothers who wanted to be with him, look at him, listen to him. It was a very gratifying time for our young Saint. He was able to teach his young brothers in

Christ the importance of the holy and committed life.

The Lord came for St. Gabriel on February 27, 1862. He had suffered enough. He had developed into a solid role model for youth for generations to come. It was time for him to go to the Kingdom where he could continue to work for the Lord in a more powerful way.

Almost immediately, graces and favors were poured down on those who prayed for the intercession of the precious little brother who had been taken from the people too soon. Mostly the people who knew him from Isola di Gran Sasso and Morrovalle prayed for his help. His old friend, Maria Pannechetti prayed for his intercession. But then word spread, by word of mouth and petitions began coming from far and near. His popularity spread all over the center of Italy. The Cause for his Canonization was opened in Terni in 1891.

✟✟✟

Our first encounter with St. Gabriel of the Sorrows came when we began our research in Lucca, Italy for the chapter and television program on the life of St. Gemma Galgani for our book and TV series, *Visionaries, Mystics and Stigmatists.* While we were in the dining room of the Giannini house in Lucca, where St. Gemma spent a great deal of her life, Mother Vittoria, custodian of that shrine, and longtime sister of the Passionist Order dedicated to St. Gemma Galgani, pointed to a painting on the wall of the dining room. We could see the strikingly handsome face of a young man whom she identified as St. Gabriel Possenti. He had bold, black eyes which seemed to pierce through to our hearts. Yet on his face, there was a mischievous smile which made us wonder when we first looked at the portrait, but after having researched his life for this chapter and television program, we find that this is the boyish quality of St. Gabriel which made him so lovable and human. He could be mischievous at times, and Mother Angelica says that's a good sign that he was not born a Saint; he had to work for it.

At any rate, Mother Vittoria began sharing the connection

of St. Gabriel,[8] in the life and spirituality of St. Gemma Galgani.

He came to her at a time when she was suffering badly, both physically and spiritually. And this would be the time when he would come, when someone needed a lift, some help, a smiling face. In her case, she had just come back from living with an aunt. Things in Lucca had been so bad, her family could not afford to take care of her. So when this aunt was willing to take her in and show her the finer things in life, her brother and sister-in-law jumped at the invitation.

For Gemma, things were not going well. The aunt wanted to expose her to the more worldly life, which Gemma didn't want any part of. The aunt even had two men come and ask for Gemma's hand in marriage. This was more than Gemma could stand. She had committed her life to Jesus as a virgin. She was an extremely beautiful girl. We agree that Jesus deserves the best. And Gemma was certainly the best (as was Gabriel, who was also very charming, both physically and personally). But when you bring to light a beauty like that out in the world, people are going to go after her.

So in addition to being extremely uncomfortable by her surroundings, which were very material, she began to experience tremendous pains in her back and spine. She complained to her aunt about her condition; the aunt allowed her to return to Lucca. Now, Gemma loved her relatives who were well off. She was just a fish out of water. When she returned to Lucca, her spirituality benefited from the change, but her physical plight became frightful. The pains in her back were so bad, she was bent over. In addition, she began suffering attacks of meningitis; her hair began falling out; she lost her hearing, and to make the situation completely intolerable, her legs were paralyzed. Nothing could be done for her. Doctors and family were completely puzzled. A kind lady came to visit and left a little booklet on the life of *Venerable Gabriel of the Sorrows,* who had

---

[8]Venerable during the life of St. Gemma

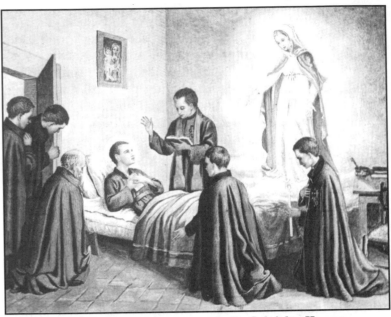

Above: *Our Lady comes to take St. Gabriel to Heaven*
He died of Tuberculosis on February 27, 1862

Above: *Original tomb of St. Gabriel in the*
Shrine of St. Gabriel - Teramo, Italy

died only thirty some-odd years before, and was already a Venerable.[9] Well, considering her physical and spiritual state at this given point in her life, about the last thing she wanted to read about was a Venerable called Gabriel of the Sorrows. She had sorrows enough of her own.

But had she read about Gabriel, she would have known that it was just situations like this, where he loves to get your attention. Her situation went from bad to worse, when she was attacked by Satan. The father of lies tried to convince her that if she would turn to him, he would take away all her pains, her fears, and would make her happy. She was in such bad shape she was ready to give in, when she had a thought, a desperate thought, but nevertheless a thought. Call on *Venerable Gabriel of the Sorrows*. As soon as she even contemplated this, a wave of peace came over her. Then, when she was tempted a second time, she called on him one more time. She was now filled with such serenity, she jumped for the book about his life. She wanted to find out more about this brother who had just saved her from such agony. She immersed herself in the little book on his life. She re-read it. She couldn't get enough of it. She didn't want to give it back to the lady who had left it to her. That evening, St. Gabriel appeared to her in a dream, and told her to be good and he would come back to see her.

Life was one failed operation upon another failed operation, pain upon more pain. Then one day, she had a thought. she would like to enter the *religious* life. It was the Feast Day of the Immaculate Conception in 1898. When she received permission from her confessor to become a religious, she had another dream of *Venerable Gabriel*. He told her to simply make her vow to be a religious, and say no more about being in a religious order. Then, he gave her a heart (worn by the Passionists) to kiss. After which, he placed the heart on her heart

---

[9]Venerable - first title given in the process of Canonization - first Venerable, then Beatified, and finally a Canonized Saint

and called her *"Sister."* The next day, Gemma made her vow and received Holy Communion.

But although her soul was at peace, her body was still racked in pain from her inflictions. It got so bad a priest had to be called in to give her the last Sacraments of the Church, including her last Holy Communion, her Viaticum. But that was not the Lord's plan at all. He just wanted to introduce her to her brother in Christ, St. Gabriel, still Venerable at the time. One of the Sisters of St. Zita gave her a novena to St. Margaret Mary Alacoque, to whom Our Lord Jesus had given the gift of the Sacred Heart Devotion.[10] St. Gemma vacillated, beginning, stopping, beginning again. Finally, on February 27th,[11] she began the novena of St. Margaret Mary in earnest.

That very evening, around midnight, she was awakened by the sound of rosary beads rattling in someone's hand. She could hear a very soft, hushed male voice intoning the prayers, the Our Fathers, the Hail Marys and Glory Be's. She found herself praying in cadence with her uninvited guest. Softly the voice asked her if she wanted to be well. She begged for his help. She was told to pray with faith to the Sacred Heart of Jesus, and he would return each evening and they would pray together. He allowed her to see him. It was the same brother who had given her the patch of the Passionist heart and placed it on her heart. It was Venerable Gabriel.

St. Gemma Galgani was to be closely related with St. Gabriel Possenti of the Sorrows, throughout her life, which was only another three years after this last apparition. We believe that they were together when Gemma cast off her earthly coil and entered into the Kingdom of Heaven. There are many reports of St. Gabriel appearing to those who have asked for his favors, and many instances of miraculous intervention by the young Saint.

---

[10]Read about St. Margaret Mary in two of Bob & Penny's books, *Visionaries, Mystics and Stigmatists,* and *This Is My Body, This Is My Blood, Miracles of the Eucharist Book II*
[11]February 27th is the day St. Gabriel of the Sorrows died.

There is a very interesting account told by Fr. Camillus, C.P. in his biography of Saint Gabriel, which has to do with the beginnings of the opening of the Cause for his Canonization. We have to preface this story with the fact that all religious orders were suppressed and dispersed by the government. That meant that the monastery as well as the tomb of St. Gabriel at Isola di Gran Sasso had to be abandoned by the Passionists, and put in the hands of the Lord, through the local people who lived there. In 1892, Fr. Francis Xavier, recently elected General of the Passionists, who had been a classmate of St. Gabriel, was given the divine inspiration to open the Cause for the Canonization of Gabriel. Well, the first thing they had to do was identify the body. In order to do that, they were required to go to the monastery clandestinely to identify his remains. Secretly, not telling a soul outside the community, they began the trip to Isola di Gran Sasso.

All went well until they were near their destination. They began to see people lining the sides of the road, dressed in their finest, heading for the monastery. The Friars had no idea what was going on, until they reached the entrance to the Church. It was blocked and barricaded by townspeople who dared them, under pain of very serious consequences, to attempt to take away the body of their Saint.

The commission could not determine how the townspeople knew anything about their activities, as they had maintained total secrecy regarding their plan to go to the monastery. When they asked how the people knew they were coming, no one person could tell them how they were informed. Word had passed among the people that grave robbers were coming to take away the body of their Saint, and they were to stop them. When the friars explained what they were doing, trying to make Brother Gabriel a Saint, the people were taken back somewhat. They respected the Passionist fathers, but they were firm in their commitment to protect the remains of the Saint.

A compromise was reached. They were allowed to go into

the church and examine the remains of Gabriel Possenti. But they were not allowed to take any part of the body away with them. This was agreed to by all. However, the townspeople did not trust the friars 100% and so they named a delegation to witness the exhumation and identification of their little Saint-to-be, and prevent any improprieties. Even with that, hundreds more showed up at the appointed time of the exhumation than were supposed to be there. The Passionists tried to get the excess people to leave the church, but that was not about to happen. So they finally gave in and all the people witnessed the identification of the little Saint.

He was beatified by the Church on May 31, 1908, and then canonized at St. Peter's Basilica on May 13, 1920. At his canonization, there were forty-five cardinals, two hundred eighty bishops and sixty-one thousand faithful gathered at St. Peter's Basilica in Rome to pay honor to this new and very necessary Saint for the Youth.

We were given the gift of a more personal encounter with St. Gabriel Possenti this summer when we went to the place where he spent the last years of his life and is buried, Isola di Gran Sasso in Abruzzi, Italy. It is a mountain place, which would make sense because it was the seminary where he did his studying. We are not sure what we expected. We thought we would have to really search out anything that would be significant with regard to this young Saint.

When we go to Europe before the pilgrims come, we usually visit any shrine we're going to write about, or make a television program about, before the pilgrims come. We don't want to take a chance on bringing them somewhere which is not really a shrine, or a shrine which is not truly a place they would like to visit. In effect, while we're gathering information on the Saint, and videotaping the shrine to use in our program for EWTN, we're also checking it out to see if it's worthwhile to bring the pilgrims. You would be surprised at many of the places we visit that would not be acceptable to bring pilgrims.

Left: *Chapel of St. Gabriel Possenti in Teramo, Italy*

Below: *Tomb of St. Gabriel Possenti in Teramo, Italy*

Very often, when we're doing this, we go on what we call *l'Aventura*, because we just don't know what we will find or how much traveling we will have to do to find *anything*. This is what we fully expected when we left Corinaldo, the birthplace of St. Maria Goretti, and traveled down the Autostrada for Abruzzi, and the burial place of St. Gabriel of the Sorrows. We should have realized we were wrong when our Italian driver, Aldo, [a saint of a man who has been with us first as bus driver, and then as private driver for over ten years] told us he had brought his family to the shrine of St. Gabriel in Isola di Gran Sasso. We were happy to hear that, but only because we felt we wouldn't get lost trying to find the shrine. We really had no idea what we were in for.

As soon as we got off the Autostrada and entered the smaller road leading to Isola di Gran Sasso, we began to see signs for a sanctuary. It didn't say what sanctuary, but we had to believe it had something to do with St. Gabriel. There were a lot of signs and there were a lot of cars heading in that direction, even though it was a weekday, Friday. As we approached Isola di Gran Sasso, we could see this huge mountain peak, reminiscent of Mont Blanc in size, but without the snow. Remember, this was July in the Appenine mountains in central Italy, not the Alps mountains. Aldo told us that the huge expanse in front of us was Gran Sasso, the mountain. He also told us we would not have to climb the mountain. The shrine was at the foothills of Gran Sasso, thank You Jesus. As we entered the grounds of the shrine, we were completely surprised at the huge tribute paid to this little Saint about whom we in the United States have either heard nothing, or very little.

Needless to say, Bob and Brother Joseph ran all over the shrine, taking photos and videotaping while Penny went in search of a Passionist brother or priest who could give us some information on the shrine and the Saint which we could add to what we already knew. You will get to see all the exciting buildings they have there and the programs especially for the youth which are a major part of their ministry, when you see our television program on Saint Gabriel. But for the purposes of the book, the most important thing about this grand remembrance given to this Saint is how important he is to the Italian people, and, actually, to all of Europe. The week after his Canonization, May 21, 1920, Pope Benedict XV, who had a great devotion to the Saint, declared St. Gabriel of the Sorrowful Virgin, *"a new patron of youth for the Universal Church."*

This is one of the main reasons we wanted to include him in this book on *Holy Innocence*, Role Models for the young. At the shrine, they have retreats and workshops for the youth of the world, year round. While it's true that the summer is when they get the bulk of their young people visiting, what with school being closed for that time, it is a total year-round ministry for the young. In this small corner of the world, the Lord is alive and well and working with His people, especially the future of our Church, the young.

St. Gabriel is considered a powerful intercessor especially for the youth. He has been named *Co-patron of the youth of Italy.* Today more than ever, we need Saints as Role Models for our young people. The attacks are most furious, separating our youth from their families. Parents, pray to St. Gabriel of the Sorrows to help intercede for you with the Lord, asking His mercy on your young people who are separated from you physically, spiritually or emotionally. Pray for his help in bringing you and your young ones together. The future of the world and the church are our young people. We need them; Jesus needs them.

Young people, you have a friend in St. Gabriel Possenti. He was a regular person, just like you. He loved all the things you love; he understands the struggles you may be having in your own special world. He is just like you, but he loved and chose Jesus and Mary rather than the world. You can do the same. Try it; it's not that hard! Remember, always, you have Powerful Friends in High Places. ***Praise God!***

Above: *St. Maria Goretti Saint of Purity*

Below:
Shrine of St. Maria Goretti in Corinaldo, Italy

Below:
Room of the birthplace of St. Maria Goretti in Corinaldo, Italy

Above:
The birthplace of St. Maria Goretti in Corinaldo, Italy. On October 16, 1890, she was born here of Luigi Goretti and Assunta Carlini.

St. Maria Goretti

The little White and Crimson Rose of Jesus

The name of Maria Goretti has a special place for me. I would judge that most everyone in my generation has grown up having heard the story of the little crimson and white Rose of Jesus, St. Maria Goretti. Her story inspires such emotions in us, such a desire to bring ourselves to Jesus and His Mother Mary as pure buds, ready to flower into whatever vocation They desire for us, whether it be religious, lay people or as in the case of little Maria, Saints who gave their lives as martyrs rather than stain their immortal souls by committing a sin. And in that way, Saints like Maria Goretti become role models for young people in these modern times.

We know the story of Maria Goretti with surface knowledge. She is famous for what she obviously did, die rather than allow her relationship with Jesus to be compromised by giving into a sexual temptation. This is the obvious cause for her Sainthood, much as St. Maxmilian Kolbe's obvious reasoning for Sainthood was taking the place of a fellow prisoner in the death cells of Auschwitz during the Second World War. But these are only the apparent. There is so much more to each life which calls for us to venerate them as special servants of God, true role models. We have written about St. Maxmilian Kolbe in two different books, trying to tell the story of this powerful man in the Church.

There were two other virtues of St. Maria Goretti which are so subtle, they get lost in the shadow of giving her life. One of them was selflessness. She cared more about her eternal soul than her bodily safety. And possibly even more than that, she cared about the soul of her attacker more than her own life. As we get into the woeful story of her life and death, we can't help but realize that part of the reason for her determination not to give into Alessandro Serenelli was for his salvation.

Maria Goretti was a good little girl, a pure little girl. At eleven years old, she had such a love relationship with Jesus that she would rather die than allow her chastity to be compromised, rather die than take a chance on breaking relationship with Jesus. But how can that be? How could she possibly understand what path her Yes to Jesus would take her down? We're not talking about St. Agnes or St. Cecilia or Saints of the early Church who gave up their lives for Jesus. This is the Twentieth Century. She is a product of this century. Where have we gone, how low have we become, that our young people can't possibly understand how a girl from their own century could sacrifice her life for her morals?

Girls as young as eleven, are "sexually active," have become pregnant, have had abortions often with help of their own mothers, in many instances, and those who did not die on the abortionist's table, have died of AIDS in many instances. We're at a time in our society when there are virtually no morals being taught or practiced either in the classrooms of our schools, in the pulpits of our churches, or in the homes by the parents of these children. Our schools are giving children condoms and parents are putting girls on the birth control pill. We're being taught safe sex in an effort to avoid the spread of dangerous diseases and to keep the world population down. Last on the list of priorities is the prevention of the spread of moral decay of a civilization, which in its final analysis will be much more deadly than any physical disease our children may contract.

Maria Goretti is definitely a contradiction in terms. She is surely a paradox. She could not possibly exist in this, the last decade of the Twentieth Century, the end of the second millennium, and yet she is a product of our century. Either she is completely out of sync, or we are condemned for the apathy we portray to our children by our behavior. Either Maria Goretti is wrong or we're wrong. Is it possible that we could be wrong?

✝✝✝

But we're getting way ahead of ourselves. To begin at the

beginning of this short, but brilliant life in the Lord, we have to go to the far north and east of Italy, to the Marches, the harsh area around Ancona and the Adriatic Sea. For those of us who visit the Holy House of Loreto, it seems a most pleasant place to be. The month we usually choose, July, is not yet hot. The warm breezes off the Adriatic make it a most desirable time to visit our Lady of the Holy House there. But that's July in Loreto. Not too far away in Corinaldo, where our little Saint was born, things are not quite the same. The winters are brutal. The howling winds coming off the Adriatic Sea pound against the rock-hard land, making it next to impossible to do any work on the farms.

If this is not enough, the Spring and Fall bring hard rain and flooding, ruining any small amount of crops which could be planted. No matter how hard the farmers tried, this was not a good place to make a living. For the parents of Maria Goretti, Luigi Goretti and Assunta Carlini, it was home. They had lived here all their lives, as had their parents before them and their parents before them. But that didn't make their lives any more bearable. It was just consistent.

And this is where our little Saint was born on October 16, 1890. She was the second living child of the Goretti family, the first boy having died as an infant. She had an older brother, Angelo, and would have more brothers and sisters as time went on. When we wrote of the Little Flower of Lisieux, St. Thérèse, we said Saints beget Saints. Maria's mother in particular, Assunta, was a saintly woman. She had no formal education, but she was taught powerfully by her Church and given, we believe, infused knowledge by the Holy Spirit. This love for God and her Church was passed on to her children, especially little Maria. She was baptized the day after her birth. Assunta did not want to have her child carry the stain of Original Sin any longer than necessary.

Under the tutelage of Assunta and Luigi, Maria grew up a very selfless, giving girl. She cared more about pleasing others

than for her own comfort. Little things had great meaning to
Maria. Perhaps because the family had always been and would
always be financially very poor, she had no great need for
possessions. They were not available to the family; Maria didn't
think about them. Instead, she tried to do whatever she could to
make her family's life more pleasant. She was a very normal girl,
enjoying games and running through the fields. But her mother
noted a strong spirituality in her from an early age. It never left
her; it just became more intense.

Little Maria and her family lived a happy life in Corinaldo,
but they were always on the edge. The land was too small and
difficult to farm. Luigi did the best he could, but it was not good
enough. He insisted that he could not take care of his family in
the proper manner under these conditions. He argued they would
have a better chance in some far-off land, perhaps the big city,
Rome. The grass was always greener somewhere else. Besides,
anything was better than they had. Assunta, on the other hand,
was determined to not leave the place of her birth and that of her
children, especially for a decadent place like Rome. But Luigi
was resolved to give his family a better life. To make his case
stronger, their very close friends and neighbors, Domenico and
his sister Teresa Cimarelli, were planning to leave also. This
gave Luigi courage to convince Assunta that they and their
children should leave Corinaldo and head towards Rome.

The lure of the big city always attracted the people from
the farms. But it had not helped those who left in most instances.
Although there was work, very often there was no life. The
wages were just above slave labor; the living conditions were
impossible; the whole family had to work in different factories.
The work of St. Don Bosco in the slums of Torino in the last fifty
years of the Nineteenth Century had been proof positive that
there were no streets lined with gold in the big cities, only
heartbreak and very often the breakup of families.

But Luigi had his way. Had he allowed himself to be more
influenced by Assunta and less by his neighbors, things might not

have turned out the way they did, for him, his daughter Maria, Assunta and the whole family. They headed for Rome, carrying all their life's possessions in a little cart. They traveled in a caravan with their neighbors, two little carts carrying two families in search of their dreams. It took a number of weeks to get to Rome. They had much time to think about the path they were taking. The prospect of a new adventure filled them with excitement of how it was going to be. That is, until they finally reached Rome.

It was a complete disaster, worse than anything they had ever imagined, either in Corinaldo or on their trip. They were completely lost. The city was huge, overpowering. They were swallowed up in its decadence. They looked for something familiar, to which they could relate. There was nothing. They were very depressed and disappointed. Searching for something, anything, they latched onto another pipe dream, tales of beautiful farming country in an area called Nettuno, between Rome and Naples, near the Atlantic Ocean. It sounded magnificent; there was the possibility of share-cropping, which meant that the workers would farm the owner's land, and share in the profits after all expenses had been taken out. It could work, but it would be difficult. However, with a strong man like Luigi, who had a great need to make things better for his wife and his family, the challenge was right up his alley. So they left the crowded city of Rome and headed south towards Ferriere, a small village near Nettuno.

As rocky and hard as the land of Corinaldo was, the Pontine Marshes, the farm which the Gorettis and the Cimarellis worked was wet and murky and swampy. They were far from home. This was not at all what they had envisioned. The swamps were filled with malaria germs; but they hadn't known that. What they did discover was that nothing around them lived, no trees, no animals, no living thing. But they had to make a go of it. As a positive, they did have wide stretches of land on which they could plant, rather than terrace farm, which they had to do in Corinaldo.

It was indeed a challenge for the family. The farm and houses had been abandoned for three years. They had to put it back together and get a crop planted. Their home was above a dairy farm, thus the nickname it had been given by the local people, *the cheese factory.* Assunta and the children worked on making the house livable while Luigi worked the fields, digging ditches for irrigation. Although Luigi prayed hard while he worked, and we are sure he had the help of the Angels, he took on more than he could handle. He would not hire help, because he had no money to pay them, although he could have offered them part of the crop. To give him the benefit of the doubt, he was probably so much in debt, he felt with this first crop he would be able to pay off most his debts. However, he didn't consider that the very air he breathed was poison, and the water he drank was contaminated. He worked himself too hard. In short order, he became very sick. This caused a decision to be made, which proved disastrous for the family, and ultimately fatal for Maria.

At the very time Luigi became too ill to work and had to be confined to bed, the owner of the property, Count Mazzoleni came to inspect his land. He saw Luigi in bed sick, and the crops laying in the field going bad, not gathered in the barn as the Cimarellis had done. He took matters into his own hands, and hired a man, Giovanni Serenelli and his son to work as partners with Luigi, to bring in the crop. So the very thing that Luigi wanted to avoid was thrust upon him. Control was taken out of Luigi's hands, and in addition the family was exposed to strangers living with them, which Assunta probably would never have allowed in their home. Little did they know, when this was done that the son of the man who became his partner was Alessandro Serenelli, the young man who would be the murderer of Maria Goretti.

Things seemed to work out reasonable well, at least that

first season. Luigi tried as much as he could to work side-by-side with the other two. Alessandro was a strapping youth of eighteen, with a great deal of strength. He did much work and spent most of his off-time in his room, reading, as it was learned later, books about violence and war, rape and lust; just the things Assunta did not want her children to be exposed to. But nobody knew this until it was too late, and the situation was forced upon them because Luigi was so sick.

During this first three years at the farm, Maria adjusted beautifully, as Assunta predicted she would. She became mother's helper in every way she could. She was always good, according to her neighbors. She was always neat and clean, but never vain. The children of that area were all poor, so she had no problem keeping up with the Joneses.

As soon as she became old enough, her mother gave Maria the chore of going into Nettuno to do the shopping for the family. This was how Maria became well-known to the local villagers. Everyone loved Maria, whom they affectionately called Marietta, or little Maria. After her death, many of the local townspeople recalled various good things about Maria which they had noted. She was always very polite and friendly. She never tarried, but took care of her errands and returned home to help her mother. She was adorable, and many of the storekeepers would give her little treats. They noticed however, that she never ate these little goodies in their sight, but put them in her pockets. When questioned, she would say that this cookie was for her sister, and this sweet for her brother. She always considered others, more than herself. Even on the day of her death, she was more concerned about her attacker's soul, than her own well-being.

Luigi's health went steadily downhill, to the point where he could not even go out with the other two to work. He contracted the diseases which were prevalent in the area, malaria and meningitis. Towards the end of April, 1900, Luigi took to his

Above: ***Home of St. Maria Goretti in Ferriere, Italy***
She was mortally wounded by Alessandro Serenelli here,
trying to protect her purity.

Left:
The location where St. Maria
Goretti was mortally wounded
in her home.

Right:
St. Maria Goretti,
mortally wounded,
received her
Viaticum from the
same priest who
had given her
First Holy
Communion six
weeks before. At
this point she
forgave
Alessandro.

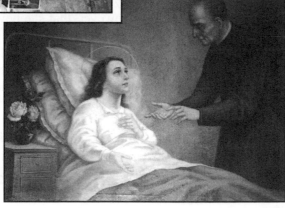

bed for the last time. His condition deteriorated drastically, so badly that they called the priest to give him the Last Sacraments of the Church. He was not aware at first that he was dying. Every time he came out of his coma to find the family and neighbors praying over him, he was shocked. But towards the very end, he whispered to Assunta, *"Go back to Corinaldo....Assunta, go back...to Corinaldo."*[1] And then he died.

Luigi was able to sense trouble before he died. Perhaps the Lord had given him special Graces to warn his dear wife of the impending danger to the family, there at the Pontine Marshes. Nothing good had come of their move. He had been wrong, and was paying for it with his life. Did he know, at that moment of death, the evil which threatened his beloved daughter? Was that why he was trying to warn Assunta to return with the family to Corinaldo?

Whatever the case, Assunta felt it was impossible to return to Corinaldo. The oldest child was only thirteen, not old enough to take on the role of a man. They had nothing to get them to Corinaldo, and nothing waiting for them there except the community they had left. For some reason, they were never able to get out of debt. She had hoped that they would be able to build a little nest egg, which would finance them back to Corinaldo. But it didn't happen. There was some talk about Giovanni Serenelli hoarding some of the crops which he sold on the side, and keeping the profits. Luigi had suspected it, but could inever substantiate it.

Assunta felt the best thing for the time, was to relieve Luigi and continue working in the fields, and pray the Lord deliver her and the children from this life, which she had never wanted. She knew she was in a bad situation; she just wanted to get out. She had to take Luigi's place in the fields, in order to maintain the partnership. Otherwise, everything would have

---

[1]In Garments All Red - Fr. Godfrey Poage 1950

gone to Giovanni and Alessandro, and Assunta and the children would have become servants for their room and board. She did not complain, but became uneasy that she had to leave her girls alone at home when she and her son Angelo went out into the field. Maria was around eleven at this time, and stayed in the home to care for the youngest daughter, Theresa. So the mother Assunta took on the role of the father, and the daughter, Maria, took on the role of the mother.

✟✟✟

Maria had always been a happy girl, a selfless girl. We are hard-pressed to find any accounts of Maria being even the slightest bit naughty. You have to remember that the people of the local villages surrounding Ferriere and Nettuno knew Maria from the time she was six years old when the family first arrived in 1896. Maria had always been her mother's right hand, helping in every way possible. She would go into the village to shop for the family. She would speak to the neighbors on the way in and on the way back. Any little act of kindness she could perform, she immediately did. Everybody knew her and loved her. They would do anything for her.

A great example of this would be, when she wanted to receive her First Holy Communion. If she had a passion in her life, it was to be as close to Our Lord Jesus as humanly possible; and she knew the only way she could do that was by receiving His Body and Blood, Soul and Divinity in Holy Communion. In those days, the normal age for a person to receive First Holy Communion was twelve. But Maria, at age eleven, pressed her mother to allow her to take instructions. Now you have to realize that Maria could neither read nor write; she had no formal education. All she knew about God was what her saintly mother Assunta had taught her, and what the priests had taught in church.

There were many obstacles to her receiving First Holy Communion, the least of which was she had no training. But Maria had found a woman in Conca, a few miles distant, who would teach her. She promised Assunta she would get all her chores finished and then walk the miles to and from the home of the lady who would help her.

Assunta tried to explain that there was more to it than that. She couldn't have a white dress or slippers. None of the outer accouterments were available to this extremely poor family. Maria didn't care a bit about those things; she just wanted to receive the Lord. She wasn't concerned about how she looked. She had never had a white dress and slippers. Why should that be an obstacle?

So Assunta helped as much as possible. Sometimes she would bring Maria to Conca for her lessons.[2] Other times she brought her to Nettuno to the Passionist priests so she could learn the Catechism and make her first confession. In addition, there was a priest who came through to Conca preparing the children for First Holy Communion. For eleven months, Maria, with the help of her mother, and all God's Angels, in the form of priests and well-intentioned instructors learned what she needed for that special time with Our Lord Jesus.

As the time drew closer, Assunta had misgivings. How prepared was Maria? She asked the local priest to make the decision. After speaking to Maria, the priest said to Assunta, *"Be at ease, good mother. Your daughter is very well prepared. Put away all your vain fears and confide her to Mary Immaculate. Place her under the Virgin's protective mantle and have no fear."*[3]

Now as the special event was upon them, Assunta's fears went back to how her little girl would be dressed for First Holy Communion. Her fears were unfounded! When the time came for her to receive, it was like the gift of the Magi. Assunta dressed Maria in a red dress. Neighbors came forward and

---

[2]In Padre Pio's life, we learn of his first teachers being good men in Pietrelcina, whose major qualifications were that they knew how to read.

[3]In Garments All Red - Fr. Godfrey Poage 1950

supplied slippers, a veil and a crown of flowers. Assunta allowed her to wear her earrings to complement the outfit.

The day she received her First Holy Communion was the Feast of Corpus Christi, the Body of Christ. Maria was full of anticipation. She did a beautiful but unusual thing. Before she left for the church, she went to every member of her family, including Giovanni and Alessandro Serenelli, and asked forgiveness for anything she may have ever done to offend them. She did the same with the neighbors.

Where did she receive this special Grace? We believe she had a special relationship with Jesus and His Mother Mary that we'll never know about. We believe when she went to the church that day, the whole Heavenly Family, including all the Angels and the Saints, were there with her.

None of her biographers make mention of the effect that *"first kiss of Jesus"*[4] had on Maria. But we have to believe that the feelings described by St. Thérèse of Lisieux, the Little Flower, who had died just a few years before Maria received her First Holy Communion, would apply here. St. Thérèse wrote:

"At last the day came, that greatest of days for me; even the tiniest details of that visit to Heaven have left their imprint on my memory, not to be described.

"What comfort it brought to me, that first kiss Our Lord imprinted on my soul! A Lover's kiss; I knew that I was loved, and I, in return, told Him that I loved Him, and was giving myself to Him for all eternity.

"And now....something had melted away, and there were no longer two of us - Thérèse had simply disappeared, like a drop lost in the ocean; Jesus only was left, my Master, my King."[5]

The only hint we have of the profound impact this

---

[4]St. Thérèse of Lisieux called her First Holy Communion her first kiss from Jesus

[5]Autobiography of a Soul - written by Saint Thérèse

encounter with her God had on Maria, was that when all the other children ran into the sacristy after Mass to thank the priest, Maria remained behind in the church, lost in the embrace of Jesus, Mary, the Angels and the Saints. We're told that the only sad part of this momentous occasion was how much she missed her father. We have to think that he was there, embracing his daughter with the entire assemblage from Heaven.

Just to recap, when Maria began instructions for First Holy Communion, she had not yet reached eleven years old. But she felt an urgency to go through the preparation stages so that she would be able to receive Our Lord when she did. Did the Lord give her infused knowledge that she would need His strength in the Eucharist for the days ahead? This need she felt to begin her lessons was manifested, right after her father's death. Did Our Lord allow Luigi to come to his daughter and whisper in her ear the importance of doing it right away? Did he warn her she would need this strength when the fatal day came, less than six weeks later?

When her father died, Maria threw herself into the work of supporting her mother. She knew how she was needed, and that there was no time for the luxury of mourning her dear father, whom she loved with all her heart. So she did what she had to do. But we wonder if her pillow wasn't wet each evening with the tears she shed for the loss of such an important person in her life.

She carried out her duties without complaint and with great cheerfulness. But those who knew her claimed that her eyes had lost their luster. She was never the same after the death of her father. It was as if part of her life were taken from her and she would never be the same.

Maria's problems with Alessandro did not just begin after she received her First Holy Communion. To the contrary, she could feel the lustful burning of his eyes on her from the time the Serenellis first moved into the house. The question that came up so many times after the fact was *why* didn't she tell someone when it first began? The answer is that the Gorettis were in a no-win situation. Had Maria said anything to anyone, to her mother or to Alessandro's father, it would just have made their situation that much worse. Even if she were believed, it would have created insurmountable problems. And so she remained silent.

During the cause for her Canonization, this question came up again and again. Why did she not tell someone? It was hard for anyone to completely understand how selfless this child was, how she always thought of everyone else before she ever considered herself. This was just another of those instances. Only it would prove to be fatal.

✢✢✢

The Final Scenario

We will speak later of Alessandro Serenelli, his life, his problems and his conversion. For this chapter, we want to concentrate on our little Saint and go through the events leading up to July 5, 1902, the day Maria Goretti was brutally murdered.

As Maria advanced in years, she began developing into a beautiful young lady. In addition, the inner beauty which could be seen by everyone who encountered her was blinding. Add to that the fact that she was obviously taken by Jesus. She was the flawless child of Jesus, and that made her even more desirable. Anyone who is unattainable is most desirable. This was the case with Alessandro Serenelli. He had made advances to her, which she was able to ward off. He threatened to kill her if she told anyone what he was doing. She was very uncomfortable with him, but felt she could handle the situation. However, it began seriously getting out of hand at this time.

Under normal conditions, Alessandro worked out in the field and Maria stayed at the house, taking care of her infant sister and preparing meals for the family. However, whenever he could, he managed to get back to the house where he would attempt to make her engage in sexual activities with him. She had been able to control Alessandro.

Then one day Assunta did not feel well. She asked Maria

to take her place out in the field. Maria jumped at the chance to get out of the house and work in the field. She forgot to consider, however, that Alessandro would be there. While they were working in one section side by side, he came over and grabbed her arm. He was angry. His eyes were crazy. He was talking what she conceived as gibberish. Finally, she understood what he wanted, to have sex with her. She summoned all her strength, broke loose from him, and ran into the fields, hiding behind a large hedge. She stayed frozen to the spot until lunch time, when she went with the others into the house. He kept giving her that look that warned her not to say a word, or he would kill her.

After lunch, when they all went back into the fields, she hid out in the barn for hours. A real sense of panic entered into her heart. She, who had never been afraid of anything, became frightened whenever she was near him, or whenever she was alone. Her beautiful eyes were dead. The special smile which lit up a room, was no more. She was in a constant state of panic. She looked for ways to avoid him during the following week. He looked for ways to be close to her, alone with her.

Saturday, July 5, 1902 - It was a very hot day in the Marshes. Back home in Corinaldo, Maria could just envision the coolness coming off the mountains and the Adriatic Sea. But here, mugginess prevailed. Everyone was tired. It had been a long week. Today was just like any other workday. Only now, Maria was working back in the house, taking care of her sister, preparing the meals and the like. After lunch, everyone went out into the fields. Maria was mending a shirt Alessandro had given her. She was at the top of the landing outside the house, praying for a gentle breeze to relieve the heat.

Alessandro had been working a plan in his mind. He was ready to put it into effect. He told Assunta he had to go back to the house for something, a tool. Remember, she knew nothing about what was going on. As he stealthily worked his way back to the house, he checked to see where his father was. He found him sleeping under the steps. The baby was asleep on the porch; Maria was at the top of the landing.

Alessandro went past Maria into his room and took out a nine inch stiletto knife, which he covered with a handkerchief. He went past her again to the storehouse where he sharpened the blade. Then he called Maria to come into the house. She had made a rule not to be with him anywhere alone. She would not go in. She asked why he wanted her to come inside. He repeated his command. She refused again. Finally, he came out on the landing and dragged her into the house. He brought her into a room and bolted the door. She began screaming, but the sound was drowned out by the sound of the thrasher and the children working with Assunta.

Maria had been through this routine with Alessandro before. But this time she could see a fire in his eyes, straight from hell. He kept trying to put her down and grab at her clothes. She continued fighting with him. He yelled at her: "Give in, Maria. Let me have you, or else..." and for the first time she saw the huge knife. Fear shot through her heart. She knew this was dangerous. She continued to fight with him. This was not working according to his scenario. "I won't take no for an answer. Either you give in or I'll kill you." Still Maria fought for her life. "Why won't you give in to me?" She cried out, ***"Because it's a sin. God forbids it. You will go to hell, Alessandro. You will go to hell if you do it."***[6]

We can picture the rage of Satan that was manifested on the face of this young man. This was the one thing Satan did not want to hear: *Don't talk about hell. This has nothing to do with hell. Don't bring that into it. It's just two people doing what comes naturally. Don't you dare bring morality into it.* But Alessandro wouldn't give up. He was really possessed by Satan at this time. He raised up the knife and threatened her one more time. She cried out, ***"Alessandro, let me go! Let me go!"*** He

---

[6]Marietta - the Story of Maria Goretti - Giovanni Alberti CP

continued to hold the knife over her, threateningly. She realized this was the moment of truth. He was on top of her. She tried to free herself from him. She couldn't. She yelled out *"No! I will not, Alessandro, no!"*

Violent anger and hate took over the body and soul of the young man. He began viciously striking at her with the long, sharp knife. He never stopped. He yelled illegible curses at her all the while. He just continued until she was covered with blood. He had stabbed at her stomach and chest fourteen times. She was writhing in pain, moaning, but not speaking. Even through all of this, she tried to keep herself covered. Finally, Alessandro, completely drained of strength, lifted himself off her, threw the knife behind a closet and staggered into his own room, locking the door behind him.

St. Maria Goretti lay there for no one knows how long. Eventually, the baby began crying as a result of all the noise that had taken place. Alessandro's father, Giovanni, woke up and wondered where Maria was. Then he heard her moaning and calling for help. Assunta could see that the baby was alone on the porch and in danger of falling. She ran into the house at the same time that Giovanni called out for her. Maria had begun to crawl out of the house when Giovanni saw her. At first there was confusion as to what happened, followed by action to try to save her life, followed by indignation and anger when Maria told her mother who had stabbed her. Neighbors who had come with rifles and pitchforks tried to break open the door of Alessandro's room, but to no avail. The Count entered and told them to wait for the police to come and arrest Alessandro, which they did. He feared they would kill Alessandro.

Little Maria Goretti, fearless Saint of Our Lord Jesus, role model for youth for years to come, suffered for twenty hours before she gave up her body and soul to her Master. An ambulance came to take her to the hospital in Nettuno. The neighbors gathered around her stretcher as they carried her out of her house; they knew they would never see her again. She traveled along a bumpy and dusty road to Nettuno. This was a familiar road to her. She had gone back and forth many times in the six years she had lived in Ferriere.

When the ambulance arrived at the hospital, Maria was more dead than alive. She was only concerned about where her mother would sleep, as she was not allowed to sleep in the hospital. A small crowd of people had gathered at the emergency entrance to see the little heroine who had staved off the lustful animal. She tried to maintain a pleasant look, but it was just impossible. The ride had taken its toll on her. But even then, her innocence and beauty could be seen through the pain and agony.

At about the same time Maria was being carried up the stairs of the Orsenigo hospital, two mounted police were dragging Alessandro into the local prison in Nettuno. So the crowd was able to have a real time of excitement. Nothing like this had ever happened before in this little area. They would talk about it for years to come. Almost everyone knew Maria from her frequent visits to the town, and they spent part of the evening remembering what a beautiful and special child she had been.

Maria went through a long night of suffering. After the doctors did whatever they could, they wrapped her in bandages and brought her back to her room. Her mother was sent out to get some rest. The nurses kept a vigil with the child. We don't know what went through her mind during that night as she woke in fits. From the screams which came out of her mouth, she was reliving the dreaded event with Alessandro. The following morning, Assunta returned to the hospital with the Chaplain, who would give Maria her Viaticum, her last Holy Communion. And as if the Lord had planned it, he was the same priest who had given her First Holy Communion less than six weeks before.

The priest did something which in retrospect, he had to do before he could give her Communion, but which was very important for the Cause of her Canonization. He asked her if she forgave her attacker, reminding her how Jesus had forgiven His killers. She looked like an Angel, as she placed her hands on her breast and forgave Alessandro. She said: ***"I, too, pardon him. I, too, wish that he come some day and join me in Heaven."***[7]

Maria Goretti, champion of Chastity, died in holiness that hot summer day in 1902 in the hospital in Nettuno. She was eleven years old. She was buried locally and remained there until 1929 when the Passionist Fathers asked Assunta's permission to place her body in the Sanctuary of the Basilica of Our Lady of Grace in Nettuno. She has been enshrined in that church ever since.

Assunta obeyed Luigi after the death of her daughter. She took her children with her and returned to Corinaldo. There were times when she wondered if she had been stronger, if she had stood up to Luigi, if the Cimarellis had not wanted to leave Corinaldo, or if they had not followed them, if Maria would still be alive. But then she realized as the years unfolded and the sanctity of her daughter was brought more and more into the public eye, this child was martyred for a reason. She was to be the champion of purity and chastity, long after her death. She was to be a role model for these last days of the Twentieth Century when she would be needed the most. Maria Goretti was beatified in 1947 as a Martyr of Purity. Less than three years later, she was canonized by the same Pope, Pius XII.

At her Canonization on June 24, 1950 in St. Peter's Square in Vatican City, Pope Pius XII, whom we believe will one day be raised to the Communion of Saints, said of the occasion:[8]

"The concourse of the faithful come here for the occasion, exceeds anything that has ever been witnessed at any other canonization. You have been lured here, We might almost say, by the entrancing beauty and intoxicating fragrance of this lily mantled with crimson whom We, only a moment ago, had the intense pleasure of inscribing in the roll of the Saints: the sweet little martyr of purity, Maria Goretti.

---

[7]In Garments All Red - Fr. Godfrey Poage 1950
[8]Speech given by Pope Pius XII at the Canonization of St. Maria Goretti

"But why, beloved children, have you come here in such countless numbers to assist at her glorification?

"...why does this story move you even to tears? Why has Maria Goretti so quickly conquered your hearts, and taken the first place in your affections?

"The reason is because there is still in this world, apparently sunk and immersed in the worship of pleasure, not only a meager little band of chosen souls who thirst for Heaven and its pure air - but a crowd, nay, an immense multitude on whom the supernatural fragrance of Christian purity exercises an irresistible and reassuring fascination.

"...During the past fifty years, coupled with what was often a weak reaction on the part of decent people, there has been a conspiracy of evil practices, propagating themselves in books and illustrations, in theaters and radio programs, in styles and clubs and on the beaches, trying to work their way into the heart of the family and society, and doing their worst damage among the youth. (Oh, if you only knew, your Holiness)

"Dearly beloved youth....tell me, are you resolved to resist firmly with the help of Divine Grace, against every attempt made to violate your chastity?

"You fathers and mothers, tell me - in the presence of this vast multitude and before the image of this young virgin who by her inviolate candor has stolen your hearts...in the presence of her mother who educated her to martyrdom and who, as much as she felt the bitterness of the outrage, never complained about her daughter's death and is now moved with emotion as she invokes her - tell me, are you ready to assume the solemn duty laid upon you to watch, as far as in you lies, over your sons and daughters, to preserve and defend them against so many dangers that surround them, and to keep them always far away from places where they might learn the practices of impiety and of moral perversion?

"Finally, all of you who are intently listening to Our Words, know that above the unhealthy marshes and filth of the

world, stretches an immense heaven of beauty. It is the heaven which fascinated little Maria; the heaven to which she longed to ascend by the only road that leads there, which is, religion, the love of Christ, and the heroic observance of His commandments.

"We greet you, O beautiful and lovable Saint! Martyr on earth and Angel in Heaven, look down from your glory on this people which loves you, which venerates, glorifies and exalts you.

"...In you, through Our hands, the children and all the young people will find a safe refuge, trusting that they shall be protected from every contamination, and be able to walk the highways of life with that serenity of spirit and deep joy which is the heritage of those who are pure of heart. Amen"[9]

✞ ✞ ✞

St. Maria Goretti, Saint of Purity, Saint of Youth, Saint of the Twentieth Century, is a role model for chastity in our world today. Her sacrifice can be used by those who follow as an example of how to live life to the fullest in Christ Jesus. Her life can be a triumph of good over evil, or it can be a waste. That, my brothers and sisters, is completely up to us. ***Praise Jesus!***

---

[9]In Garments All Red - Fr. Godfrey Poage 1950

Left:
*The Shrine of
St. Maria Goretti
at Nettuno, Italy
on the seacoast.*

Right:
*Assunta Goretti
The Mother of St. Maria Goretti
She was present at the Beatification
of the daughter, April 28, 1947 in
St. Peter's Basilica*

Below:
*Canonization of St. Maria Goretti
St. Peter's Square
June 24, 1950*

Alessandro Serenelli - *Murderer of Maria Goretti*

After having written the account of the murder of the little Rose of Jesus, St. Maria Goretti, it is somewhat difficult to write about her murderer, Alessandro Serenelli. However, in this book, we are writing about many sinners who have been involved in the lives of many Saints. This sinner was the cause of the death of our little Saint, Maria Goretti. In a larger sense, he may have been the catalyst who brought her sanctity to the eyes of the world, even though it was through violent and satanic means. Maria Goretti was a Saint, but we might never have known about her and her Sainthood if it had not been for the circumstances by which she was brought to our attention. Alessandro played a major part in our knowing about Maria Goretti. And in an even greater sense, God triumphed through the conversion of this sinner.

Alessandro's life was much different from Maria Goretti's in one sense, and much like hers in another. They were both born in the same section of Italy, near Ancona. He and his father moved from the Marches to the area of Nettuno, where they were put together with the Goretti family by Count Mazzoleni who was the landowner. They lived in the same house and worked on the same land, Alessandro in the fields and Maria in the house. But that's about where the similarity ends.

Alessandro's mother had been committed to an insane asylum when he was but two years old. She stayed there for the rest of her life and died in the asylum. One of his brothers was committed to the asylum as well. After his mother's internment in the asylum, Alessandro's father abandoned him. He spent the next fifteen years in transit, being dispatched from one relative to another, a cousin here, an aunt there. They did not want him, and he resented them. He never knew the love of a mother or father. He never had anyone to hold him and speak softly to him.

At about twelve, he went to work with stevedores on the docks and aboard ship. These were his role models; the worst possible example for a young man, but no one cared about him, and for him, they were a source of survival. They were his family, as much as he would ever know. His language became the language of the stevedores, which is limited at best, and foul at worst. His casual conversation consisted of a raft of vulgarities and curse words.

He was reunited with his father, Giovanni, when he was fifteen. By this time, the die was cast. Although there is nothing in writing to substantiate, most likely the reason his father took him under his wing was that he was getting on in age, close to sixty, and needed a strong young man to help him get work. When he was introduced to the Goretti family at Ferriere, he wanted no part of them. He didn't speak to them, avoided the children except Maria, and his motives were not honorable where she was concerned.

Alessandro did not socialize with his father as well. He was a loner. He spent his off hours in his room reading lurid and violent books. He took to hanging lewd pictures all around his room. One day, accidentally, Assunta went into his room and found these pictures. She didn't dare take them away for fear of being accused of invading his privacy. However, she warned Maria and the other children to stay away from the room.

✞✞✞

Alessandro had vile and corrupt thoughts towards Maria from the time she began to develop into a young lady. His reading material didn't help at all. He fantasized often about getting Maria into compromising situations where he could have his way with her. It went from fantasy to obsession, to the point where he thought of nothing else. On July 5, 1902, Alessandro determined he would play out his fantasies with her. He went out with Assunta and the children to work in the fields, but then went back into the house on a subterfuge. He began to put his sick plan into effect. However, it didn't work according to his plan. Maria didn't react according to the script he had written in his mind.

She would not come into the house when he called her.

She had always been a feisty girl where he was concerned. He always wondered why she hadn't been as nice to him as she was to everyone else. Maybe she could read his mind, he thought. Whatever the case, on that hot summer day, he decided he would have her. He dragged her into the house and proceeded to try to take her clothes off and rape her. She fought harder than he thought she could. He couldn't understand why she wouldn't give in to him. It just didn't make sense.

Now, you have to understand where he was coming from. His world was completely different from most. He lived a life completely foreign to anything we would understand. He did not at this time, look at Maria Goretti in the same light that everybody who knew her did.

According to every report we have read on what happened on that fateful day in July, 1902, Alessandro lost complete control when she said he would go to hell if he raped her. We have to believe he was completely possessed at that moment, and when the name of God was mentioned, he just lost it. The Satan in him raged so violently, the young man attacked what he judged to be the source of his anger. In the months to come, when he was placed on trial, he was found sane and *knew* what he was doing, we can agree with that. But what he did was so hideous, so violent, so satanic, we believe he had to have lost control at that moment.

Alessandro hid out in his room. He knew they were going to come for him. Or did he think as long as the door was shut, he was safe? The police came, and threatened to knock down the door. He finally allowed them in, but never admitted to having done anything wrong, even though they found his bloodstained shirt and pants in the room. Also, while he had tried to wash his hands with the pitcher and bowl in the room, there was still blood to be seen on his hands, as well as on the pitcher and bowl and towels hidden in the room.

Getting Alessandro out of the house and to the police station was a touch-and-go situation. The police had to protect him from the local people who wanted to kill him. They all loved Maria; they had seen what happened to her before the ambulance came. None of the townspeople could understand how anyone could have committed such an atrocious crime. They wanted to give him some of what he had given Maria.

The soldiers handcuffed Alessandro and dragged him between their two horses as they galloped to the prison in Nettuno. He was held there for some time, but was moved to a prison in Rome for fear the local people would do him harm in Nettuno. At his trial, he denied any involvement in the crime. Finally, he admitted his guilt but claimed to be insane, and used his dead mother and brother as examples. However, his arguments were considered lame at best, and lies at worst. Alessandro was sentenced to thirty years in prison because he was a youth. He was sent to a penitentiary in Sicily.

For the first eight years, they thought maybe he was a little crazy. He didn't seem angry about being in prison. The only time he went into a rage was when a priest came to see him; it was about the year 1910. He just went crazy. He began screaming at the priest, blaming the Church for all his problems. If Maria had not been taught the way she was, none of this would have happened. According to him, she would have given in to his advances, and he would not have killed her.

The priest tried to calm him down, but the more he talked about God's Mercy and Maria having forgiven him before she died, the worse Alessandro got. He actually lunged for the priest. If the guards had not interfered, he might have killed the priest, and just compounded his situation, because then he would have been tried as an adult rather than a juvenile, and would, most likely have been given a death sentence.

The priest was completely shaken as he left Alessandro. He tried to console him. "Soon, Alessandro, you will want me. Maria will see to that."

Alessandro continued to rant. "Never! I'll never want you, never!"

The priest's statement proved to be prophecy. Alessandro was not the same after his visit. He couldn't sleep; he couldn't eat. He became very nervous. Then one night, while the rest of the prison was in the dead of sleep, a piercing scream came from Alessandro's cell. He shrieked for the guards. They came running, sure he had been killed. When they looked at him, he was nearly irrational. He mumbled words which didn't make sense. Finally, he calmed down and told them of Maria's vision to him. In his own words: "I saw her! I saw her! I saw Maria dressed in dazzling white gathering beautiful lilies in a garden and handing them to me. As I took them from her outstretched hands, they were transformed into small lights that glowed like candles. Call the priest! Bring me a priest!"

The guards made fun of him. They made some malicious jokes and left the cell, laughing. But Alessandro was not to be deterred. He knelt on the floor of the cell and wrote the following note:

"I am deeply sorry for what has happened. I have taken the life of an innocent girl whose one aim was to save her purity, shedding her blood rather than give in to my sinful desires. I publicly retract the evil I have done and beg pardon of God and of the stricken family. One hope encourages me - that I also may one day obtain God's pardon as so many others have."

Signed - *Alessandro Serenelli* - November 10, 1910

From this time on, Alessandro began his conversion. Not much is known about his remaining nineteen years in prison. We're told he was a model prisoner, and testified till the end of his life that Maria had appeared to him.

After his release from prison, he was considered an outcast by his people. Although he had confessed his crime, and as a result, all doubt as to the authenticity of Maria as Saint was abolished, with possible exception of some Devil's Advocates in Rome, he was still the killer. Nothing he could do would wipe that out. He went to the tomb of Maria Goretti after his release from prison and prayed there. Then he went deep into a self-imposed solitude, from which he did not come out until he was asked to testify at the Cause for the Beatification of Maria Goretti.

As we mentioned, there were some Devil's Advocates in Rome who were asking questions like, "Why didn't she tell someone about his advances?" "Did she provoke him?" "Why did she hesitate before pardoning him?" The people were very upset because Rome was taking so long. But Alessandro put all those questions to rest when he testified before the tribunal. He told them he was to blame completely for everything that had happened. Maria was without guilt; she was entirely innocent of any wrong-doing. That was all they needed. They proceeded with full speed, and although it took them another ten years for the Beatification to actually happen, the people trusted that all obstacles had been removed.

Alessandro returned to Corinaldo in 1937. Assunta had gone back with her children soon after Maria had died. She worked in the Rectory of the church there. Alessandro went to her on Christmas Eve of 1937 to ask her forgiveness. Assunta looked at this man who had taken her precious rose from her, who had changed her life forever. She began to weep, but the words that she uttered were just what we would expect from the mother of Maria Goretti: *"Maria forgave you, Alessandro, so how could I possibly refuse."*

The following morning, Christmas Day 1937 found Assunta and Alessandro entering the church together, hand in hand. They went to the front of the church. Alessandro turned to the congregation and confessed his sin. He begged God's forgiveness, declaring that Maria and Assunta had forgiven him.

The last public appearance Alessandro Serenelli made was on April 28, 1947 at St. Peter's Basilica in Rome, for the Beatification of Maria Goretti. Alessandro was there with Assunta, and Pope Pius XII for that occasion. Maria was canonized less than three years later on June 24, 1950. Alessandro was not there for her Canonization.

From what we have been able to gather, he retired to a Capuchin monastery in Ascoli Piceno, where he worked as a gardener for the rest of his days. He died on May 6, 1969 after a painful illness caused by a broken hip and arm. According to the Capuchin fathers, his last words were: "I am going to be again with Maria in Paradise." *Praise Jesus!*

Above: *St. Margaret of Castello*

Above: *Shrine of St. Margaret of Castello in Citta di Castello, Italy*

Above: *St. Margaret of Castello's heart is united with the hearts of the Holy Family*

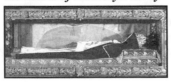

Above: *St. Margaret of Castello in Glory*

Left: *Incorrupt body of St. Margaret of Castello*

Blessed Margaret of Castello
Saint of the unwanted

In a world where life is cheap and death is expedient, where women are killing their own babies in their wombs, where the span of ones life is dependent on another's evaluation of his/her quality of life, where the Culture of Life has been overtaken by the Culture of Death, it is time for a Saint, a Saint of the unwanted. Although Margaret, at this writing has only been declared a Blessed, and has not been officially declared a Saint, those who *knew* her and *pray* to her for her intercession *believe* she is a Saint. She is not only, because of her affliction and history, a *Saint of the unwanted*, not only of the *unborn* (who most certainly are unwanted), but she was known in her lifetime and after as Margaret, *Miracle Worker*.

For those who consider themselves too ugly, too fat, too skinny, too short, too tall, too this or too that, read the astounding heartbreaking most glorious story of a miracle working in this little Blessed whose body is still there in the church where she was laid to rest, for us to see and believe - in God's Love for us all, that He died for us all and that He is with us, manifesting His Power to save us.

We have said, when writing Mother Angelica's story, that she is the greatest contradiction in the Twentieth Century. Writing some of these chapters, we find ourselves thinking of her and the great sign that she is to all of us, of God's Love for all His children who say Yes. To quote Mother Angelica, *"If we will but do the ridiculous, God will do the miraculous."*

Stay with us, as we travel to Italy and trace the life of another Dry Martyr,[1] Blessed Margaret of Castello.

---

[1]A Dry Martyr, according to the late Archbishop Fulton J. Sheen is a Martyr who does not shed blood for the Faith, but suffers day in and day out for Mother Church. As you read, see if you agree with us that Margaret of Città di Castello is such a Dry Martyr!

The Renaissance,
        a time of glory and devastation,
                of honor and dishonor,
                        a time of selfishness and selflessness.
We are in Italy, and we find ourselves again in the area
which gave birth to Renaissance, the Region of Tuscany.

In the Twentieth Century, a Martyr, Blessed Edith Stein,
as she was awaiting her death in Auschwitz - the infamous Death
Camp, said, *"Someone will have to pay for this."* She went to
her death, not only for her fellow Jews,[2] but for the Nazis who
were killing her and the other Jews, saying if she did not pray for
them, who would!

In the Thirteenth Century, the Renaissance was definitely a
time of the haves and the have-nots, the privileged and the
underprivileged, the time of the greatest Saints and the worst
sinners, it was a time of cruelty and compassion. This story
encompasses all these positives and negatives with more to boot.

Did you ever notice how evil begets evil, and good begets
good? Our story takes place in a time of greed, pride and power,
with these evils compounded by man's unquenchable thirst and
gluttonous appetite, devouring and consuming all three. There
was a war between the old order and the new; man had lived
through the devastating period called the Dark Ages and in his
quest for happiness threw out the baby with the bath water. With
Renaissance and the fulfillment of the needs of the ego, the self,
neighbors coveted their neighbors' land and fought their
neighbors, leaving many dead on both sides to achieve an empty
victory.

When books are written, like *Dante's Inferno*, the
characters are monstrous, and because the author writes in the
fiction mode, we think they are fictitious when more often than
not, they are real. And so it was when Dante wrote this book; it

---

[2]Blessed Edith Stein converted from Judaism to Catholicism and became a
Carmelite Nun. More on Edith Stein in Bob and Penny Lord's book:
Martyrs, They died for Christ.

was a commentary on real times about real people. We know that *pride* is the root of all evil. During this dark, supposedly enlightened period of the world's and the Church's history, there was no place for imperfection. As with today, *obsolescence* was the key word. If it is not new and shiny, throw it away. If when we read a sonogram we see the baby is deformed, well abort it! Thank God, in the time of Margaret of Castello there were no such instruments.

We seem to be writing about this period quite a bit in this book, but I think it is God again saying, in time of need, He sends *Saints and other Powerful Men and Women*[3] to save His Church. We read about Pope Innocent III in the life of St. Rose of Viterbo, and here he is again. The Pope is reorganizing the papal states from Rome to Ravenna. Our little Margaret's story begins in a papal state called Massa Trabaria. As it was right in the center of the other newly formed papal states, it was important strategically to forestall attacks on states to the north and south.

Now, in Massa Trabaria there was the town of Metola, where a castle surrounded by a fortress loomed high on a mountaintop, affording clear vision of impending attacks from any side. It is believed it was first erected to be a lookout for advancing Saracens troops. When wars between the states began to occur, this fortress became a strong defense and offense. Now, this fortress had a reputation of being impenetrable, surrounded as it was on three sides by a cliff unscalable by man or beast, and by archers poised atop the fortress' walls, bows arched, ready to attack any soldiers trying to cross the deep, broad moat which protected it on on the fourth side.

Although the fort could not be penetrated from without, because of betrayal within, it was captured and occupied by the state of Gubbio for twenty five years. When the captain (or podesta) of Massa Trabaria died, his son Parisio was chosen to take his place. His first act was to storm the fort and recapture

---

[3] titles of two of Bob and Penny Lord's books

the castle for the state of Massa Trabaria. Needless to say, he became a hero, not only of his state, but of all the papal states. He and his wife from that time on inhabited the castle and enjoyed the privileges and respect due him now as a lord of Massa Trabaria. Parisio was a wealthy man, having inherited a small fortune from his family, and not only that but from the sale of trees, for which this region was also famous, and if that was not enough, the taxes he mercilessly extracted from his serfs.

Parisio was known to be a man one did not challenge, as he was harsh, unloving, and totally unsympathetic to the plight and needs of those less fortunate. He was haughty, prideful, arrogant and a fearful sight when he walked among the townspeople and the soldiers in his garrison. His wife, Lady Emilia was completely subservient, complacent, and compliant, yielding to his slightest command. One day Lady Emilia informed her husband she was with child. Emotions she never perceived in him rose to the surface. His thoughts turned to planning for the upcoming event. He decided it would be more accessible and conducive, for the many personages he was going to invite from Massa Trabaria and the surrounding papal states, if they held the banquet celebrating his son's (he already had determined the baby would be a boy) birth and baptism, at the foot of the mountain. Now, Parisio was not religious in the least, but he had quickly agreed with his wife to have their son baptized when she mentioned it would not look good for an up and coming Lord of an important papal state, like Massa Trabaria, to not have his newborn son baptized.

It was decided that not only would the celebration take place there, but Lady Emilia would give birth to the baby at the bottom of the mountain. The serfs and the troops in the garrison would celebrate simply in the fortress on top of the mountain and the gentry sumptuously in the town. For the serfs and soldiers the food and drink would be plentiful but modest. But for the invited dignitaries, only the best wine was imported for the occasion, to wash down the pheasant being served.

Even though they were not to be part of the grand festivities, the serfs all joined in the excitement of the joyful event that was to come to pass, joining in, preparing for that great day. To show you how high were his hopes and plans for his son-to-be-born, Parisio was already preparing lessons and mapping out strategies that his son would use someday to annex less protected and therefore more vulnerable papal lands. One day, as he was passing by the blacksmith, he said, *"It won't be long before you will be making a suit of armor for my son, eh?"* To which the smith enthusiastically answered, *"Your Excellency, I'll make him the finest suit of armor in all Italy!"*

A baby is born

There is a hush in the town and on the mountain top, in anticipation of the new little lord, as if time is standing still waiting for the signal to rejoice! Lady Emilia went into labor. The candle bearers were ready to brighten the castle, symbolizing the light that had come into their lives. The serfs stood ready to ring the bells! The baby was born, but no lights, no bells tolled, only deadly silence. A baby girl was born; that was one blow. The infant was rejected immediately by her parents; she was not only a girl, she was deformed! She was not a pretty baby; if her parents were to believed, she was ugly. She would never reach full height, they determined as she already showed signs of being (as her parents later told her) a midget! Her right leg was shorter than the other, and so they knew she would be lame, as well. Believing God had punished them, one week later, they discovered they had not seen the total chastisement; the child was blind! What a disgrace, they thought!

The word went out that the baby was very sick and was not expected to live! As it was impossible to keep them from becoming aware what had transpired, the serfs and soldiers in the fortress were told that this was not something to be broadcast. As Parisio was known for the merciless cruelties inflicted on those who disobeyed him or got in his way, it was fairly *fait-*

accompli[4] that no one would know of the little girl who had come into this cruel world, and cruel it would turn out to be, making this reaction and subsequent action a kind one in comparison.

The local parish priest, Father Cappellano insisted the baby be baptized! And as was the custom of that time was that the baby be baptized in the cathedral, he faced very stubborn opposition; Parisio flatly refused. But when his wife reasoned with him, he reluctantly agreed - on one condition, Lady Emilia's maid would bring the baby girl and have her baptized. The heartless twosome (parents) even refused to name the child; they left it up to the maid, with only one admonition, she was not to bear the name Emilia!

The maid took the baby to the cathedral in Mercatello. When the priest asked the name of the infant, the maid cried out, Margaret, meaning *pearl*. Although her *outer* visage was not what the world would call beautiful and extraordinary, her soul would prove precious and priceless, truly a pearl. The maid returned. All the serfs hoped the parents' hearts would soften, after all she was their child! But that was not to be the case. Not even when the priest who was teaching the child told them how extraordinarily bright she was, his best student, did that melt their hearts of stone.

She was a friendly, loving child, in spite of her parents' obvious disdain of her, knowing all the citizens of Metola by name, whether child, man or woman; and this considering she was blind was quite a feat! Everyone in Metola began to love her and looked forward to her visiting them, which she did by herself. She knew how to get to everyone's home; there was only one place she was forbidden to visit and that was the rooms of the palace which her parents occupied.

She was the little pixie of the fort. But at age six that was to come to an end. Visitors came to the palace to visit her parents. It seems the nurse absentmindedly forgot to tell little

---

[4]an established fact

Margaret to stay in her room; to compound the situation, she carelessly left the door opened. As was her custom, Margaret went to pray in the palace chapel. She met up with one of the visitors, who, seeing her condition, asked her compassionately if she was blind, to which the child responded she was. When little Margaret addressed her respectfully as *Your Ladyship*, the woman asked if she was blind how did she know she was a Lady. Margaret responded, *"You speak just like my mother."* Just as Margaret was about to divulge *who* her mother was, Margaret's nurse retrieved her just in time to avoid a disaster! But not without her parents finding out how close they had come to being exposed as Margaret's parents.

Parisio came up with an idea, as Margaret loved to spend hours praying in the chapel, he would build a cell next to the church and place Margaret in the cell where she could pray as a recluse. His wife, to give her some credit, could not believe he would place his own child in a prison, because that's what it amounted to, especially as she was only six years old! When she protested the Church would never allow a child to become a recluse, he retorted angrily, it was not their affair, but his! He used every lame excuse for his inhumane treatment of his daughter; she will be happy to have the privilege to pray all day long, so close to church; in this way she will be safe, after all it was not prudent for her to walk around the fort, she could get hurt. Finally, his mind already made up, he told his wife he was commissioning a mason to begin constructing the cell tomorrow.

Margaret begins the Way of the Cross

The church Parisio was referring to, his wife soon found out, was not the chapel of the palace, but one in the forest called The Church of St. Mary near the fortress of Metola. As it was the parish church of the serfs and it was one quarter of a mile from the palace, with only some very rocky paths leading to it, guests would not be likely to visit and discover the little cell and inquire what was within. The tiny cell was constructed with a very low ceiling, so it did not take long to finish, and Margaret's days of sunshine, visiting all her friends in the fort, playing with other children, were over. The little prisoner was thrown into the cell, and without showing any emotion her father ordered the doorway to be walled up. My God, he had confined his own daughter to a hot box in the summer and an unbearable ice box in the severe winter, a punishment grown men have not been able to survive after five days.

Although all the men in the garrison and their wives were enraged, no one said anything, afraid of the mad retaliation of their lord. Only the timid, gentle soft spoken pastor Father Cappellano spoke up, pleading for the child, accusing the father of being heartless. Parisio responded by threatening to rip out the priest's tongue if he said another word. Father Cappellano warned the two, mother and father, if they persisted in carrying out this act against God Himself, He would vent His righteous anger against them, ending with may God have mercy on their souls.

Margaret's mother's lady-in-waiting, Lady Gemma and her husband Leonardo were dismayed over their helplessness to do anything for little Margaret. Leonardo said he wished that Margaret would have been incapacitated mentally as well as physically, this way she would not suffer knowing her parents did this foul, inhuman deed. His wife scolded him. He continued, protesting that with her brilliant, active mind as she gets older, she will feel greater and greater pain knowing her parents cared so little for her, they would deprive her of even a meager, quasi-normal life.

Lady Gemma confided, Margaret already knew her parents did not love her. When Lady Gemma had kissed her and told her she loved her, Margaret said, "How can you love me? My babbo[5] and mamma said that no one could love me because I am such a freak!" Margaret continued, when she asked her parents what a freak was, they responded that other children were not

---

[5]a loving name for her father, like we would say Daddy

midgets, crippled, blind, hunchbacked, lame and ugly. She was all of these and more. Upon hearing this, Leonardo flew into a rage, calling upon God to strike both parents dead! His wife, Lady Gemma, pleaded with him to be silent, lest someone hear and report him. And again, as in the time of Jesus, fear kept people from doing the right thing, the Christian thing.

There was a knock on the door, just then. It was Father Cappellano. He guessed they were talking about Margaret as no one could think, no less speak of anything else. When Lady Gemma said it would be better if the little one had died than suffer knowing she would never have a normal life, never know love, a prisoner day and day out without any human companionship, the priest said how little we Christians know about our Faith. He said that Margaret knew that the reason we were born was to know God and knowing Him, love Him; and she knew that we can only know Him through His Cross, sharing His suffering on this earth. He said if she does not weaken, someday she will bless the Lord for her afflictions, for she will receive her crown of glory. He asked only that they join him in praying that the Lord preserve her, in her faith and courage in the days ahead.

When Leonardo argued the priest expected too much from such a little girl, Father Cappellano recounted, when visitors came to his room, they shared how brave Margaret had been, that she had entered the cell without shedding a tear. *"But,"* the priest continued, *"it was not that she did not feel sadness, for when I returned from speaking to her father, I overheard her sobbing, her little child's heart breaking."* Oh, she knew what was happening, but with the signal grace of the Martyrs before her, she was able to spare others from sharing her cross.

When Father asked her why she was crying, was it because she had been locked inside this cell, all alone, she shocked even him, knowing her the way he did, as she answered, *"Father when they brought me here this morning, I did not understand - because of my sins - why God let this happen to me. But now, he made it clear. Jesus was rejected by His own people, and God is letting me be treated the same so that I can follow our dear Lord more closely. And Father, I am not good enough to be so near to God!"* She became so overwhelmed with the thought that God loved her so, she could not continue.

Margaret was a normal child who grew into a normal young girl, with all the feelings and temptations that fill a young vessel, such as she, to the point of overflowing with emotions. She was hurt that her parents did not love her, but she accepted it as a gift from God for her own good. The more her passionate nature threatened to separate her from her God, the more she not only willingly accepted suffering, she sought suffering, imposing more and more mortification upon herself, fasting, and wearing a hair shirt before she was seven years old.

The years went by slowly; the only calendar she had was the change of seasons - it was spring when she heard the birds chirping outside; it was summer when the cell became suffocatingly hot; she knew it was fall, when she had relief from the blistering heat; as the days became cooler, she knew that winter with its damp, freezing cold would soon be upon her. And this is how she spent twelve years of her life, but that was soon to end.

Margaret is released from her prison!

June 5, 1305 an incident would occur which would change the course of Margaret's life - a French Pope was elected! Parisio and his council convened and discussed the gravity of the situation.   They concluded, a French Pope would not be sympathetic toward an Italian papal state in case of an attack. Furthermore, as the Pope had decided to relocate the Vatican temporarily in Avignon, France, because of threats against the Papacy by different warring factions, it would not be feasible for the Pope's troops to be made available to defend Massa Trabaria. In addition, there had been rumors that Montefeltre, a neighboring state was planning to attack in the spring.

In another place, in a tiny cell, our little Margaret only

knew that winter was passing and spring was on its way; the birds were singing outside, welcoming a new day, rays of sun were trying to force their way into the cell. Little did she know that soon she would be free from this tomb. She could hear tolling of the town bells growing in intensity. She didn't know why, but her little heart began to beat wildly; were her parents and friends in danger?

Meanwhile at the fortress, they became aware of their neighbor's bell tolling to the north; it suddenly made sense; they had been trying to warn them of the rapidly approaching threat to Massa Trabaria. Smoke filled the air! Farmhouses in the distance were burning! The castle's bells tolled now in unison with those in the distance; Massa Trabaria was under attack!

Margaret began to tremble; tears flowed down her cheeks; the villagers would be killed; her father would be in danger, as Captain of the people he would lead his soldiers to do battle with the invaders. The little Martyr fell on her knees and prayed to the Lord to spare her father, the soldiers and all the families of Massa Trabaria.

Meanwhile back at the castle, Parisio was issuing commands, readying his troops for war. Anyone refusing to fight would be hung, immediately! With his sweet words having been uttered in his usual cruel and intimidating manner, Parisio went to his wife's chamber to tell her to get ready to flee to Mercatello, where she would be safe. Lady Emilia, not totally inhuman, asked about her daughter, what would happen to her. Parisio told her to take the *"freak"* with her. When the wife enjoined that it would be virtually impossible to hide her there, he annoyingly countered with, *"Place her in a dungeon underground; she is to have no visitors!"* Troops left with Lady Emilia and a tiny heavily-veiled girl for Mercatello.

And so, Margaret traded one prison for another, as she entered the sparse, cold underground cell, her furnishings - a miserable, coarse burlap pad filled with straw which rested directly on the floor - this was her bed - and a bench. If it was possible for a prison to have been worse than the one she had spent the last twelve years, this cell was. At least in Metola, she could hear the Mass, the priest would come to visit her, to bring her the Sacraments of Reconciliation and the Eucharist. Here she was to be deprived of all that! She would be brought food twice a day; if she had any needs she had to speak up then, or wait until her jailer returned with her next meal. Under no circumstances was she to utter a sound!

Deserted once more, Margaret would inquire after her father and the soldiers; her agony was intensified by the news many were dying and her father was in great unrelenting danger. But soon, other states joined Parisio; he countered by attacking his enemy - Montefeltro; finally a truce was made between the two; the war was over! When Margaret was told the news she rejoiced; her father had been saved; the village had been spared; there would be no more bloodshed! But her joy would turn into a sorrow and pain so terrible she could not have imagined it!

In the town square, word spread that there were grey friars from Rome who were in town! The news they were bringing brought utter dismay to the villagers of Mercatello; the Pope had decided to take up permanent residence in Avignon! All the villagers gathered in church, crying out that the Lord was punishing them for their sins! At which, the friars told them of their reason for coming to their village, in the first place - there was a holy friar whom the Lord had placed in their midst who had the gift of healing. Surely, God wouldn't have done so, if He no longer cared for them!

New hope - Margaret leaves her prison!

Parisio returned from the wars, and immediately departed for Mercatello to bring his wife back to the fortress. Now, his wife had heard of the friar with the miraculous gift by this time, so when he arrived, she appealed to her husband to bring Margaret to the friar. When he protested, the mountainous terrain would be too much of a hardship for a lady like herself, she answered she would brave it, if there was the slightest chance

Margaret could be *"normal."*

Preparations were made, troops were assembled to accompany their commander and his wife, with her maid (they thought, as their faces were concealed). The heavy bolted gates were opened and they were on their way. Lady Emilia excitedly told Margaret of the friar and his gift, confident he would cure her. Margaret's father even said they would all go to confession and receive Communion before they went to the friar. Parisio even called her *"dear child"* when he asked her to pray that God would grant them this favor. She was ecstatic; she had never had the gift of hearing her father call her his *"dear child,"* nor mention going to receive the Sacraments of Penance and Holy Communion. How loving her parents are, she thought! What a gift to at last hear these words from them!

I am sure Margaret, in her excitement, did not notice that they were the *only ones* who were in church at Mass that morning. They received Holy Communion and then with the idea of giving God time to bring about the miracle, they left Margaret in the church and went walking about the town. They were confident, because of their importance - their noble blood, if this friar could heal peasants, surely God would grant this favor. When they returned, hours later, Margaret was sitting in the church, right where they had left her, and there had been no change!

They could not take her back to Mercatello, they reasoned. Well God had not answered their prayers, they would handle the matter, themselves. Without even looking back, they headed toward the inn where they were staying and told their escort to make arrangements to leave, at once! They rode, as if they were being pursued, running their horses to the point they were frothing at the mouth; they were like criminals running from a crime. Yes, and criminals they were, the worst kind; they were running away from their own child, leaving her - blind, crippled, alone, without money, shelter; they had left her to die! And were they being pursued; I believe so, by the hounds of Heaven; only they would not allow themselves to be caught.

When her parents were about to leave her, they told her to wait for them; they would be at the other side of the church, out of the way to allow other pilgrims to approach the altar and the friar. Margaret waited, listening for the sound of their footsteps approaching; she knew that sound by heart! There were many who passed by, but no parents. When they had told her to pray for this miracle, she obeyed, but with a provision (they had not included), that it be only if it were according to God's Will.

Familiar with the chiming of the bells and their meaning, the noon bells rang, then mid-afternoon, then for vespers. Margaret could hear the rush of many footsteps hurrying into church, but not those of her parents. The day had ended! The sacristan told her she had to leave the church, as it was time to close it for the night. She asked him to help her to the door, as she was blind! He inquired then how had she come to the church, in the first place. Whereupon, she told him her parents had asked her to wait for them, and they would return; she would sit on the front steps; surely they will come, soon! Dawn gently lifted, bringing with it new hope; a new day had begun! But she could not hear her parents' footsteps; they were nowhere to be found. For the rest of her life, Margaret would listen for those footsteps!

Margaret begins a new life!

The next day she would not leave the church; first off she did not know the name of the inn; then when her parents returned, if she were not where they had told her to stay, they would be sick with worry. I do not know when Margaret came to the full realization that her parents had deserted her. She had to go through all the painful possibilities - had some former enemy recognized them and hurt them; has someone kidnapped them and was holding them for ransom? Oh, how this innocent child prayed no harm would befall those two selfish monsters who were her parents. *I don't know about you, but I am having a hard time writing about this little soul.*

As the sun began to warm her face, she had to come to the cruel possibility that her parents were not returning. A day had passed and she had not eaten, the thought came to her that she would somehow have to find a place to stay! When it finally hit her that she might have to fend for herself, it had to be another devastatingly frightening realization. Although her hovel had been just that, and her meals meager, she had been cared for, for twenty years; how would she manage? Well, it was God's business and He would handle it!

Here we have God using *who* He will, *how* He will, *where* He will! Picture little Margaret on the front steps of the church and two beggars spotting her. They were furious; this was their spot; let her find a place of her own to beg! When they confronted her, they could see she was blind. They pulled away her cloak and they could see this was no ordinary beggar; her clothes were made of the finest fabrics. There might be a reward! After much interrogation, they discovered the inn where her parents were staying. Upon inquiring, they were told that Margaret's parents and their entire entourage had sped away, the day before. Margaret could not believe they had left her behind. The beggars took her to the border guards, who verified they had passed through, hurriedly, heading toward Mercatello.

For the first time, this young, innocent girl had to come to the reality that her parents not only did not love her, *that* she knew as they had told her so many times, but they *hated* her. She cried to herself, *"I never thought they hated me!"*

As she tried to collect her thoughts and feelings, she struggled to accept this *new* development as a gift from the Lord - after all, she reasoned, her Lord had been abandoned by his friends! This is fine to intelectualize but she has been abandoned, left to die. Her head told her she was growing closer to Jesus, but the ache in her heart needed healing; she turned to God to help her forgive them. In the meantime, villagers had heard of her plight and they were not sparing their feelings regarding her parents. Would you believe she began defending them, saying after all, for twenty years they had cared for her, given her a place to live, food to eat. Now, she insisted it was time she took care of herself.

Discovering she had no money and no means to support herself the beggars began to teach her their *trade*. They not only did that, they showed her where she could wash in the town fountains, in which doorways she could sleep protected from the elements and the police who were always picking up vagrants and throwing them into prison. One night, one of her beggar friends went looking for her, to be sure she was all right; she found her huddled in a corner covered by snow. She immediately brought her to the carpenter who owned a barn, and asked if Margaret could sleep there at night. Margaret, warm and cozy, slept beside the cows and horses, happy again that she could share in Jesus' life by so doing.

When her beggar friend Elena apologized for the smell in the barn and the dirt, bitterly adding beggars have no choice, Margaret instead blessed God, exclaiming how good He is. Elena argued God had nothing to do with it. Margaret asked her to think, Wasn't it God who put into her head the first time to help her, to teach her, to befriend her, this night to come and see if she was all right? And wasn't it God who told her to go to the carpenter and ask for shelter in his barn; and was it not God who moved the carpenter to say yes?

She went on to tell her God loved her, just the way she was; that God loved beggars, that He hungers for her love and the love of all His children.

Margaret was to touch the hearts of many of the villagers. That night Elena got down on her knees and prayed for Margaret, saying, like the *good thief* before her[6] that she had sinned and deserved whatever she got, but Margaret was good and had done nothing wrong, except be born of the wrong parents. And so, as one Babe Who was born in a stable converted and changed the

---

[6]to Jesus on the Cross

hearts of many, this His little disciple would do likewise. Elena was on her way to the Kingdom!

There were, as with Jesus, those who loved her and those who distrusted her. But consistency will always prove the cut and fabric of a person better than a garment. Margaret soon won over the whole town! The wealthy looked the other way, in an attempt to avoid her; but the poor who had little for themselves offered their homes and shared what little they had, somehow recognizing the Saint in their midst. When one home was not able to provide for her, another family shared their home; and so, Margaret got to know *all* her new family and they learned how precious a gem this little sister was. It was in these humble households, among those considered marginal and unimportant that she found the most endearing gift of love, unconditional generosity and complete selflessness.

But all was not sunshine, roses and violets, there were crosses other than poverty that attacked these poor souls. Many were away from the Church; some openly attacked the Church; and although she did not let her disapproval show, it wounded her; and so she prayed. Living in cramped quarters, never enough to eat, many quarreled angrily - accusing each other, blaming each other; Margaret prayed! And a strange thing happened; everywhere Margaret stayed, change came about. Peace entered their homes and the fighting turned into loving one another. Those who shared what little they had, found their cupboards were always full. What they would soon discover, most important of all, was that God loved them!

Margaret enters the convent, only to know rejection, again.

Finally the gentry of the village went to the local Monastery, and explained that a young woman of Margaret's background and upbringing should not be tossed from house to house. And as they were handsome benefactors and quite insistent, the Prioress agreed to call a meeting with her Council to discuss the possible entry of Margaret into their convent. As she later explained: to enter a convent, a postulant must have an exemplary character, be of legitimate birth, with no physical handicaps. The Prioress came back to the benefactors and explained that although Margaret more than filled the first requirement, it was the other two which blocked her entry. Possibly they could overlook the last, but with the second, relating to her legitimacy, there could not be any compromise.

As Margaret had been quite evasive concerning anything about her background, the Nuns were doubly suspicious. Knowing they had a hot issue on their hands, they decided to put the whole question in the bishop's hands; they could always hide behind him, if things did not work out and Margaret could not enter. The bishop gathered what information he could and sent it to the cathedral of Mercatello where he knew Margaret was baptized. When the rector of the cathedral discovered Margaret was the daughter of the well-renowned Captain of Mercatello, he was both appalled and fearful; he knew what the illustrious Parisio did to those who crossed him.

The bishop simply said Margaret had been baptized and was legitimate! No name was revealed! The Nuns warmly welcomed Margaret into their community. She did not present the kind of problem they had anticipated; they would later discover one that they could not abide. Not only did they not have to care for her, the Nuns were amazed to discover she not only took care of herself and provided whatever meager means she would allow herself, she took on herself household duties, such as cleaning the rooms of the convent, washing kitchen utensils; she loved to prepare the meals and then to set the table, performing the smallest to the biggest tasks with intelligence and dedication, filled with joy and peace.

She was so happy! Without training and knowledge beforehand of convent life, she embraced the Rule of the community, with all her mind and heart, just as she had pledge as a child, to love God. She, like the Saints before her, lived according to the first rule of any vocation, obedience to her superior. As she considered the Rule the clearest way to lead her to a life of obedience and subsequently holiness, she followed the Rule strictly according to the holy founder's original vision.

Now, the community had been relaxing the Rule, little by little, pulling away from the very fabric of the charter drawn up by their founder, until it was hardly recognizable, barely perceptible and with it, the community's original charism. Although the Nuns were not faithfully adhering to the ancient Rule of their founder, Margaret was not judgmental. She had come there to become a Saint, and she was just going about, doing all she could do to fulfill that dream. But sadly, nothing changes. When Jesus came, He brought the Light, and when men stood in that Light, they could not stand to see what they had become, and rather than change they rejected Him, right up to the Cross; and so it would be with Margaret! The Nuns complained to the Prioress, who in turn, tried to reason with Margaret to come to her senses, explaining that the Rule had been formulated many years before, *at* a different time, *for* a different time. The Rule had been relaxed to *accommodate* the world, rather than to *influence* the world.

But Margaret could not come to her senses, as they saw her senses. Clearly understanding her road to the Father was the narrow path Jesus spoke of, Margaret turned to her confessor, and then crying out to God for help in her journey to Him, she promised if only He would help her, she would do her best to live up to the commitment she made to Him, many years ago in the solitude of her cell. The way to the Cross had not been easy for Jesus, and it would not be for her.

She answered abuse with love and acceptance, anger with humility and submission; she dearly loved them and was grateful to them for accepting her, but it could not be at the sacrifice of her promise to the Lord. She never by word, but rather by living example antagonized the Nuns. She painfully reminded them of how they were meant to live, and for them the price was too high.

"Everyone wants to go to Heaven, but no one wants to die."7

The Prioress told her things had gone too far, and she had to bend; she must conform to the other Nuns' lifestyle. But the little Nun, protested that her confessor had told her she was doing God's Will. The Prioress said there was no other option; Margaret must change!

Margaret went to the Blessed Sacrament Chapel and knelt before her Lord so magnificently Present and placed her dilemma before Him: If she obeyed her Prioress, she would be able to remain with these Sisters she so dearly loved, here where she could be near Him, come to pray to Him, Present to her in adoration and at Daily Mass; but should she follow what she believes is His Will for her, she will be asked to leave.

As the doors of the convent shut loudly and finally behind her, there she was out in the street, without home, the security she longed for gone; she had lost all but not all, she still had God. But you know when you are frightened, alone, do not know where to go, it is difficult, near impossible to be confident there is a God right beside you, taking care of things.

Do you notice, it is when you are all alone that the enemy of God attacks? He had her all to himself; he plagued her with all kinds of doubts and recriminations, beginning with but not exclusive to thoughts like: *"It was not the Nuns who rejected you; it was God. He doesn't love you. What has He given you in return for your faithfulness? Fourteen years in solitary confinement; and if that wasn't enough, the cruel abandonment by your parents? Compromise; that's the only way; compromise!"*

She was completely beaten, helpless and hopeless, dejected and defeated, or so she thought. Suddenly, she was at the foot of the Cross; Jesus was looking down at her, and asking, *"Will you leave Me also, Margaret?"*

Margaret lifted her cane, straightened herself as much as

7Our grandson Rob once said that.

she could; and feeling her way, she walked toward the unknown, she only knew He was with her, and that was enough for her.

A new way of the Cross

As bad news travels fast and good news is seldom noticed, the town began buzzing about the little beggar who was thrown out of the convent. But not everyone reveled in her misfortune. When one of her old friends, Maria, heard about it, she first went to the convent to find out if the rumors were true; and then hearing their side of the story, very like the one that was circulating in the town (that Margaret would not conform and follow the rules set out for her), Maria searched everywhere for Margaret to see if she needed help and listen to her version.

After looking high and low, she found Margaret praying before her sweet Lord Jesus Present in the Blessed Sacrament. Seeing her alone and destitute, Maria wept at the sight of her little friend. Maria cried out angrily against the Nuns! But instead of explaining why she had to leave, like Jesus before her, Margaret did not defend herself. Rather she defended the Nuns, sharing how grateful she was for the opportunity to have been with them, and how sorrowful she was that she was not good enough to be a Nun. Maria, saying she was good enough for them, took Margaret home with her.

Now, there were hundreds in the village who had had personal experiences with Margaret; they knew of her holiness and found what the Nuns said impossible; then there were those who had heard of her, had believed in her goodness, but now that the Nuns had rejected her, were just as ready to cast stones at her. Had she been too much for them, too? As we have seen, in this our own Twentieth Century, it is easier to follow a sinner than a Saint. If the persecution by the parents was not enough, the children overhearing their parents and following their lead, took up the slack, calling her names: *"Midget! Limpy! Hunchback!"*[8] As they could not get an angry rise out of her, they

---

[8]from *The Life of Blessed Margaret of Castello* by Fr. William R.

went on to following behind her, mimicking her, taunting her, calling out *"Here comes the Saint!"*[9]

"Father if it be Thy Will, let this cup pass from Me." Margaret thought that her cup had filled to overflowing; there was nothing that could top the anguish and agony she was suffering. But she was to learn that the cup, from which she would drink, was as deep as the need of conversion in that time, in that place and Jesus had chosen her, the most unlikely, to be the instrument He would use to bring it about. The attacks were not over. There was no escape! Even in church, women made wounding remarks, attacking her character; making sure she overheard them, sneering, *"It's the old story! Put a beggar on horseback!"* They were guilty of calumny,[10] as they continued to spread scandalous hearsay about her.

Finally Margaret's reticence to speak in her own defense, her consistent defense rather than condemnation of the Nuns, began to open the eyes of those who really wanted to know the truth. Seeing how charitable she had been, not defending herself (although it would have been normal to do so), and the contrast of the Nuns who accused her (whereas they as Brides of Christ should have been charitable), they started to take a closer look at the convent and the lifestyle of the Nuns. Public opinion, which is tenous at best, changed; the Nuns lost much support and Margaret gained the respect, once more of the town.

God has a plan - Margaret becomes a Mantellate!

[You have only to look around you, to see how, in the Twentieth Century, God changed the hearts of men - through a Pope who came from an underdog nation,[11] a Nun in far-off India who began by preparing the poor for a peaceful death,[12] and a

---

Bonniwell, O.P. - Tan Books and Publishing
[9]from *The Life of Blessed Margaret of Castello* by Fr. William R. Bonniwell, O.P. - Tan Books and Publishing
[10]a sin, as it can seriously hurt someone's reputation
[11]Pope John Paul II who is from Poland
[12]Mother Teresa of Calcutta

cloistered Nun with no background in communication, who founded the largest worldwide Catholic Global Television and Radio Network in the world.[13]

God in action, placing His instruments in a given place, at a given time - *"to feed His lambs, to tend His sheep, to feed His sheep,"*[14] God is not past doing *"the miraculous, when we are willing to do the ridiculous."*[15]

It just happens that during her hardest time, when Margaret felt unworthy, the subject of gossip, derision, ridicule, and scorn, quite alone and abandoned, with fair-weather friends turning against her, God was to console her by introducing her to a group of lay women who were members of the Order of Penance of St. Dominic, the Mantellates.

Now this Order was for women who wanted to live a more religious life but, like St. Catherine, were called to serve God outside a cloistered convent, or as with Margaret were not accepted in a cloistered community. These Sisters lived at home, serving in the world while practicing a deeper prayer life. They were privileged to wear the Dominican habit, which consists of a white tunic bound by a black belt around the waist, and a white veil draped on their heads. The only difference was that they did not wear the wide scapular of the Dominican religious, rather the Mantellates wore a black *mantella*.[16]

Some of the Sisters, seeing the holiness of Margaret and her sadness at not remaining in the convent, suggested she become a Mantellate. The Prior was upset, scolding, they should not have raised her hopes; they knew that only widows who were older were accepted. He conceded there had been times that married women with their husbands' permission were eligible, but that was the exception not the rule. A single woman applicant,

---

[13]Mother Angelica, foundress of EWTN Global Catholic Network
[14]Jn 21:15-17
[15]the authors paraphrasing Mother Angelica's words
[16]cape

absolutely not![17]   But the Sisters had what we call *Holy Stubbornness* or singleness of purpose and their arguments that Margaret was not flighty like most girls her age; and with her handicap she was not likely to cause a scandal that would cast mud on the image of the *Mantellate*, swayed the Prior; and after careful examination of her character and demeanor, Margaret was to become the first single woman to join the Order of Penance of St. Dominic.

As the Prior raised his hands to Heaven, he bestowed a blessing on Margaret, saying,

"May He Who has begun this good work in you perfect it until the day of Christ Jesus!"[18]

Margaret was at home, at last, with a family, a family she had never known but desired. When she had taken her vows, at first she was so overcome with emotion, tears of joy gathering in her eyes, she could not speak, but then, collecting her composure, her voice rang out throughout the church, *"And I do promise that henceforth I will live according to the form and Rule of the same Order of St. Dominic, until death."* Now she could fully, faithfully follow the Rule as it had been set down by its founder. No more compromise; like the Word of God, the Rule was timeless, not for a time, but for all time.

Margaret not only said the prayers required by the Rule, she recited the 150 Psalms written by David, the Office of the Blessed Mother, and the Office of the Holy Cross. As she was blind, she had to memorize all these prayers; biographers say that as with St. Catherine, it had to be through Divine intervention.

Margaret loved to meditate on the life of Jesus; but her soul would soar when she contemplated on the Incarnation of Jesus. She had to do all she could to keep her heart from

---

[17]This was the same restriction which blocked St. Catherine of Siena, but not for long; the Lord wanted it and it was done; Catherine became a Mantellate.

[18]from *The Life of Blessed Margaret of Castello* by Fr. William R. Bonniwell, O.P. - Tan Books and Publishing

exploding with joy, as she thought of God, the King of the Universe deigning to unite Himself to man, choosing to be born a helpless infant, dependent on two human beings, Joseph and Mary for His very sustenance.

After she heard a sermon on the penances practiced by St. Dominic, she asked for special permission to follow all the disciplines which St. Dominic exercised. As St. Dominic followed the advice of St. Paul who said, *"if one wished to conquer the inordinate affections of corrupt human nature and thus gain an incorruptible crown, it was imperative one practice mortification,"* she felt as she was not elderly like the other Mantellates, she could handle the extreme penances without damage to her health.

One part of the sermon which particularly made an impression on Margaret, imprinting these words on her heart, were,

"Not only did our holy Father (Dominic) scourge himself, but he did so three times a day; the first time was for any sins which he might have committed against God; the second was for the salvation of his fellowmen; the third was for the sins of the souls in Purgatory."[19]

Now there are those who do not understand the need for mortification. Because of her practice of mortification, observing the penances her father Dominic had undertaken before her, she was able to keep her body subject to her soul, rather than the other way around; and with that she received the strength needed to be faithful to the vow of virginity, she took on the day she was received into the Mantellate. Although her confessors all agreed that she led a life of purity, Margaret had a passionate nature, one that she would battle relentlessly, in her lifelong commitment to honor the vow of virginity she took at age seven.

---

[19]from *The Life of Blessed Margaret of Castello* by Fr. William R. Bonniwell, O.P. - Tan Books and Publishing. You can read more about the Poor Souls in Purgatory in Bob and Penny Lord's book: *Visions of Heaven, Hell and Purgatory.*

Seeing those who had more physical gifts than she had, and had not endured the persecution she had, the rejection and abandonment she had suffered at the hands of her own parents, rather than having bitterness toward them when they sinned, she did penance for them; and when her friend Antonina begged her to curb her mortification, she protested what she did was nothing compared to what she wished she could do to save souls.

She cried there were so many souls in danger of being lost, so many living in sin, offending God. She wept over the apathy of sinners toward God and the sins they are committing against Him, against He Who had carried their sins to the Cross, dying the most horrible death that their sins would die on that Cross, and still they sin more. She said that if by her suffering and pain she could save one soul, she would gladly relive all her days locked up in a cell, away from everyone.

Her heart bigger than the body that the Lord gave her, she was never too tired, too sick to go and console the sick and encourage the dying. The townspeople spoke of seeing her, at all hours of the day and night, visiting the homes of the needy. Although I have a deep problem with her parents, how they treated her, I have to feel sorry for them; they missed out on sharing the life of a Saint! Oh, how proud they could have been of this caring, selfless little human being who rejoiced only when she spoke to God or of God, and when she could love God through loving His children.

Margaret moves again - to a house torn by strife.

As many Mantellates were from well-to-do homes, Margaret's days living among the poor had to sadly come to an end. However she never forgot them, ministering to them as well as to the rich who were poor in another way. The Offrenducio family took Margaret into their home. They were *good* people, but not necessarily *holy* people; their knowledge of the Catholic Church and her beautiful, priceless teachings were foreign to them. On the portal over the door, it read, *Domus Pacis*, "House of Peace." But sadly, it was anything but that.

There were two families living in the villa, the Offrenducio family and their relatives the Macrettis. Now this family and their ways, were very familiar to her, as they too were of noble birth. And so Margaret found herself fitting in comfortably. She began to teach the Macrettis' only daughter *Ceccha.* Everything was going along fine, when Margaret learned the young girl had no knowledge of the Faith and began instructing her on the Sacraments, teaching her prayers, the Office of the Blessed Mother and on and on. When she discovered that the girl, now sixteen years old had not been to confession since she was a child, Margaret prepared her to go to confession and make a good general confession.[20]

Although the parents were happy that their daughter was learning the Faith, as it could only help her catch an eligible husband, noble families more disposed to young women who were religious, they had not counted on the daughter becoming so enamored of Christ, she would want to become a *religious!* Now in those days, marriages were arranged between families of the same social standing, and the Macrettis had a suitable husband in mind. Not wanting to force her to marry the young man, her father began extolling his virtues, his family, his good looks, his future, the honors he had received for having performed bravely in battle; there was no contest that this young man was a winner! Then why was there a far-off look in his daughter's eyes?

The parents began thinking back, when had this distraction toward young men begin? After Margaret arrived! They were not far off; the more Margaret spoke to Ceccha of Jesus, the more Ceccha compared the world and its promises to Him, and found them seriously shallow. She decided that she would become a Mantellate! As the girl knew trying to convince her parents was like trying to open a bolted door, she began to cry.

---

[20]General confession takes place when a penitent confesses sins, especially grave ones that he may have confessed previously, or where there is doubt about the penitnet having confessed all his sins. This is to be done only under advisement of a Spiritual Director.

Margaret volunteered to take on the parents!

Margaret was asked to join the Macrettis and their guests in the sitting room. The subject of the Mantellates came up, and the outstanding work they are doing, visiting the sick and etc. Suddenly the guests remarked how lucky the Macrettis were to have a Mantellate living with them, in their home.

The opportunity was suddenly there, Margaret jumped right in with, *"Then will you consider allowing your daughter to join us?"* A silence came over everyone in the room, overshadowing the good will that had been so present. Mrs. Macretti was the first one to compose herself and speak, trying to make light of it, she teased *"Margaret, stop joking, our daughter will never become a Mantellate."* Margaret prophetically responded, *"Indeed Lady Ysachina,[21] it will not be long before not only your daughter, but you as well will be a Mantellate."*

Everyone but Margaret laughed; but a few months later Mr. Macretti died and mother and daughter became Mantellates, and they observed the Rule till the day they died. With Mr. Macretti's death, the household broke up and once again, Margaret, the Lord having used her, moved on, to the home of the Venturino family.

There is an expression, *What goes around, comes around.* Margaret had begun life in a palace, was reduced to imprisonment in cells unfit to live in, to living on the streets, to living in squalor among the poorest of the poor, to her final home on earth, a palace! Was she happy? No! She had taken the vow of poverty; her Lord had not lived in a palace. But His little bride unhappy, He guides her upstairs to a small room in an attic of the palace. Mr. Venturino, wanting to give her a room befitting her station at first refused, but one day his wife shared how brilliant she was, correcting their sons' lessons with a knowledge of mathematics and other subjects she could not have possibly learned with her limited education. His wife volunteered, maybe

---

[21]Mrs. Macretti

she received her education from the same Source Who taught her the day before she became a Mantellate. She went on that when tested that afternoon, Margaret only knew a few psalms of the Psalter; the next morning, she began reciting all 150 psalms by heart, as well as the Office of the Blessed Mary and the Office of the Holy Cross!

Needless to say, at supper that evening, Mr. Venturino advised Margaret she could choose any room in the palace; and she happily ascended the staircase to her mansion in the attic.

One day, Margaret approached Lady Gregoria, the wife of Mr. Venturino, and asked her why she had not been able to visit the prisons, as the other Sisters had. Lady Gregoria shared it was not a fit place for someone of Margaret's station to visit; the men were very coarse. Lady Gregoria shared that she felt the same way as Margaret but never asked her husband to allow her to go, because it is such a dreadful place. She shared the deplorable conditions under which the prisoners lived, the lack of food, medicine, not even mats to sleep on - their bed the cold damp floor, she knew her husband would not hear of them going there to minister to the prisoners. Margaret started to move her lips, not uttering a word.

At supper, Mr. Venturino told Margaret if she wanted to visit the prison, she had his permission, and since he had known for quite some time that his wife wanted to go as well, she could accompany Margaret. The Ladies, from the finest homes, walked among the unwanted of the world, men who even their families had abandoned, their crimes had been so heinous; and they affirmed them telling them they were children of the King of the Universe, and as such were precious to Him. They brought not only food for their bodies, but nourishment for their souls. These fine Ladies gave them dignity; God does not make junk, and now they knew God made them.

Margaret the Miracle Worker

Miracles happened in the Offrenducio home, with Margaret prophesying and the prophecies coming about. In the

Venturino home, God was once again to use Margaret. One day, the daughter of a niece of Lady Gregoria was dying. Margaret who was the small child's godmother, was seen kneeling for hours upon hours outside the child's room, praying. At midnight the bells began tolling, calling the monks to Matins,[22] when suddenly the little girl awakened and told everyone that she had been cured by the prayers of her godmother.

Another incident was when a fire broke out in the Venturino villa; everyone came to the rescue, forming bucket brigades, passing water from one man to another, desperately trying to put out the fire, but the fire could not be contained. The fire warden told Lady Gregoria he was sorry, but there was nothing further they could do, her home was burning down! He consoled that at least it was a blessing that no one was in the upper floors. Suddenly, she remembered Margaret was in her room in the attic! She ran into the house and was about to run up the stairs when the firemen stopped her, pleading there was no hope of any survivors in that raging inferno. Lady Gregoria began to scream, *"Margaret! Margaret! The house is on fire! Hurry downstairs!"*[23] Margaret appeared at the head of the stairs and said, *"Be calm! Do not be afraid. Have confidence in God,"* and then throwing her cloak down to Lady Gregoria, she said, *"Here throw my mantella into the fire."* The firemen knelt and prayed, for the moment the cloak had touched the flames, the fire which had been out of control, was extinguished!

Margaret levitates!

So many miracles and so little time to tell you all of them. But here is one, I just cannot leave out. Justice is not always served; very often the law in nations is prejudicial and unfair. There was a prisoner who was known to use such vile blasphemous language, the prison warden would not allow

---

[22]Matins were at that time the name of the first and chief hour of the Divine Office (Liturgy of the Hours).
[23]from *The Life of Blessed Margaret of Castello* by Fr. William R. Bonniwell, O.P. - Tan Books and Publishing.

Margaret and Lady Gregoria to visit him. The prisoner, Alonzo, had been thrown into prison when his brother, who had been falsely accused, fled. The authorities tortured Alonzo unmercifully, in an attempt to find out his brother's whereabouts. After hours upon hours of the most inhumane treatment, they threw his broken body into a dungeon. In the meantime, without his earnings his wife and son became poverty stricken, and when the little boy became sick his mother could not afford a doctor and Alonzo found out the child died! He kept uttering every blasphemy against a God Who would allow this to happen; he and his family were innocent, and if He is the Omnipotent God the priest says He is, why didn't he help Alonzo and his family. He hated Him!

Upon hearing this, Margaret and Lady Gregoria were more determined than ever; they insisted they be allowed to visit Alonzo. The other Mantellate, seeing there was no possibility they would change their minds, agreed, but warned them to not mention God; it would turn him into a raving lunatic uttering the worst blasphemies! Margaret and Lady Gregoria included Alonzo on their rounds, bringing him and the other prisoners food and other necessities. Everything was going fairly well, until one day. Margaret could tell by his nervousness that he wanted desperately to spew his usual tirade of blasphemies; he looked as if he would explode if he did not let lose his anger against God.

Lady Gregoria was bathing his ulcerated legs, when Margaret rose from her chair. Her head bowed, she clasped her hands together and resting them on her chest, began to pray. We do not know, if this reminded him of how his dead son would place his little hands together and pray, or what it was, but suddenly Alonzo turned his back to them, faced the wall, and began to wail, like an animal in excruciating pain!

When he heard the other prisoners crying out, *"Jesus have mercy on me! My God! Mother of God!"* he turned around and saw the petrified look on their faces; these hardened criminals looked as if they had seen a ghost! Turning his head in the direction of what had evidently brought such fear into their hearts, he began to gasp for breath. Whereas Margaret had been standing not two feet from him, she now was in the air, 20 feet from the ground, still, tranquil, stationary, not even the smallest twitch; she remained levitated, without anything holding her up for the longest time. But then she raised her head, looking upward, and then slowly began to descend. Her face was no longer ugly; her face was illuminated; she was beautiful! A change came about in Alonzo. Margaret saw the hate that he had harbored in his heart against God and man, leaving him, and she, seizing the moment, told Alonzo that God had been waiting for this moment. On hearing the mention of God's Name, Alonzo opened his mouth to blaspheme, emptying himself of all the hurts and wounds God had allowed to happen, when instead he said, *"Little Margaret, please pray for me."*

As she grew in contemplation, these levitations grew, especially when someone was suffering. The prisoners testified as to seeing this occurrence many times. It was as if she was joining their pain with that of the Savior Who had suffered for them to the point of dying on the Cross.

Margaret goes to her eternal Home

As she grew closer and closer to going to her true *Palace* and living her much awaited life with her Lord and Savior, she more and more carefully prepared to confess her sins. Considering herself the worst of sinners, she was the greatest of Saints. She went to confession every day, not wanting to offend God in the smallest sin, and would receive Holy Communion as often as it was permitted. One day, she told her confessor that when she attended Mass, she could see the Incarnate Jesus on the altar! When he tried to put her thoughts into simple language, he asked her if she meant that she was in some way aware of the Real Presence of Jesus. To which she insisted, *"That is not what I mean. I see Jesus!"* He asked how this was possible, since she was blind! She answered she didn't know.

Her confessor continued questioning her, asking her if she

saw the Crucifix and the priest celebrating the Mass; she responded *No!* See, he insisted, you are really not seeing; you are feeling His Presence, the way someone who is blind cannot actually see but senses someone's presence. Finally, after answering all his questions, she simply said,

"Father, you have commanded me to reveal to you in confession the innermost secrets of my heart. Since I am obliged to speak, I must repeat what I have said before; from the Consecration until the Communion I do not see the priest, the crucifix, the missal, or anything else. But I do see Christ our Lord."

When he asked her to describe Jesus, she answered, how impossible it was to describe the Divine. The haunting words of a Saint who had visions of Heaven, echo once again, *"Eyes have not seen, ears have not heard what God has in store for those who love Him."*

As she approached her thirty-third year of life, her friends could see her little body losing whatever hold it had on earth, her life ebbing away before their very eyes. As her soul rose more and more toward her *Heavenly Home,* her ecstasies became more and more frequent, each vision and encounter with her Heavenly Family sapping whatever strength she had, until it was obvious the little princess of God, the *unwanted* on earth was preparing to go to her Heavenly Father Whom she had so desired on earth.

Margaret called for the Last Rites from her Dominican friars, as a daughter of St. Dominic. Word got out that their little Saint was dying. The villagers congregated outside the Venturino home and unashamedly knelt on the ground, praying and crying, for her gain was their loss. Their inconsolable grief was lifted somewhat when they began to hear the distant chanting of the Dominican friars coming closer and closer, processing with the Blessed Sacrament Whom they were bringing to Margaret for her last Communion with Jesus on earth.

He allowed her to be rejected at birth from the closest people in her life, her parents, only to create in her a holiness so profound it would lift the veils on the eyes of those who knew her, revealing not a deformed misfit, but a living, compassionate Saint who was loved beyond description. And the multitudes, whose lives she had touched, were all there to pray with her, as she prepared to go to her *Heavenly Castle* to live eternally with her *Royal Family* in Paradise. This could only be of God's design for this, the littlest of His children.

And so, all the ties that bound her on earth broken, the precious soul of Margaret, perfected by fire on earth, now soared upward, ready to kneel before the Savior Who had loved her and sustained her on her tormented journey on earth. Next stop Heaven, Margaret! The Holy Eucharist and she united for the last time on Earth; she looked up to Heaven and gave up her spirit to the Lord. It was the Second Sunday after Easter. On April 13, 1320, Margaret breathed a sigh and she no longer belonged to the earth; she became part of the holy ones.

Conflict till the end, Margaret's body is finally put to rest!

Margaret, as a Dominican was in the hands of the Dominicans who would decide how and where she was buried; only they had to contend with those who loved her and were already proclaiming her a Saint! As there was little or no money to pay for an embalming, little Margaret's body was washed and clothed, ready for burial. As coffins were a luxury only the wealthy could afford, her body was not laid in a coffin, but instead placed on a litter. Since the weather was hot and humid, the body of Margaret was, out of necessity, to be buried on the very day she had died. They brought her to the Dominican church, *Chiesa della Carita*, as she had requested. The church could not hold all the mourners, many of whom knelt outside the church during the Funeral Mass.

When the Mass was over, and all the faithful had passed by and said good by to their friend Margaret, the friars lifted the litter and were about to carry Margaret to the cloister to be interred there. A mass disturbance came about with the villagers insisting Margaret be buried in the church where they could pray for her intercession. At which the friars, exercising the prudence of Mother Church, insisted she had to pass the test of time and they could not anticipate the mind of the Church.

The friars were unbending in their adherence to the Church's ruling on this matter; the laity as stubborn and resolute, blocked the entrance to the Dominican cemetery (where she was to be buried); the pall bearers placed the litter on the ground. Only a miracle could resolve this dilemma to the satisfaction of both sides. *Why didn't you say so?* God must have playfully said.

A man and his wife had brought their daughter to the church, praying for a miracle; the child was mute from birth, and unable to walk because of a serious curvature of the spine. They almost gave up hope, as it had been impossible to carry their precious child past the solid wall of bodies blocking the way, when suddenly, like the parting of the Red Sea,[24] the laity allowed them by, and they were allowed to bring their little girl to Margaret. They carefully placed their child on the ground next to the litter. Then they knelt and began to implore Margaret for her intercession. The townspeople and the friars forgot their differences and began to pray, supplicating Margaret with, *"Margaret, you know what it is like to be a cripple. Have pity on this child. Having always been a close friend to God, and now having even more influence, will you not intercede for this child and her parents!"*

They begged; they bargained; they argued; they reasoned; they left no stone unturned, when suddenly a hush came over the crowd. They were afraid to say anything, lest the others would think they had lost their minds! It appeared that Margaret had lifted her arm and touched the little girl lying next to her. Barely a moment passed when the girl rose; and as if in a daze she began to walk. Everyone was dumbfounded, and then, the girl cried out, *"I have been cured! Margaret has cured me!"* A

---

[24]Exodus 14:21

miracle had come about! Needless to say, the Prior of the friars asked the other friars to get a coffin. Margaret was placed inside the coffin and brought into the church. The town council had all the facts investigated and verified that the girl had been crippled and mute and through the intercession of Margaret, she had been cured of both ailments.

People began swarming to the church, and miracle upon miracle came about! Margaret's reputation as a Miracle worker spread from one end of the boot to the other, bringing sunshine and with it hope! In 1600, Pope Clement VIII, commissioned a committee to look into the merits of opening a cause for the beatification of Margaret. *One Saint begets another Saint;* who should be placed in charge of the process, but another future Saint - Cardinal Robert Bellarmine. The Cardinal presented his findings but Pope Clement VIII did not live to beatify Margaret. On October 19, 1609, Pope Paul V beatified Margaret, authorizing the celebration of her Feast Day on April Thirteenth.

There are those who call her the Saint of the unborn, and I agree that she is, but if I may I would like to name her Saint of the unwanted, those whom society judges have not enough of a life to preserve, for those who are coerced into taking their own lives because they are talked out of the privilege of becoming another Blessed Margaret of Castello! We are born to become Saints; it's up to us. God has given us the means, will we choose Sainthood for ourselves and our loved ones? In our family room, we have a sign which reads, *Choose this day whom you will serve. But as for me and my house, we will follow the Lord.* Amen!

Saint Philomena

Saint of Chastity

Why are we writing about this particular Saint? Her life story is little known to man, but well known by God. This you will see clearly confirmed by the thousands upon thousands of miracles granted, down through the centuries, through her intercession. These miracles, in themselves, could fill a book.

That St. Philomena has touched the hearts of many, you need only to visit the Shrines of powerful Saints, like the Curé of Ars - St. John Vianney, and see the place she held in their hearts, a living testimony of the role the little Saint of Chastity has always had in God's Plan of salvation.

Why do we say *in God's Plan of salvation?* If you recall, although Jesus cared for the bodies of the poor souls who approached him for physical healings, he was more concerned with the salvation of their souls. We will not only be speaking of the healing of the body brought about miraculously through her intercession, we will speak of the role she wants to play in the salvation of souls. Whereas, we know our Saint mostly for the miracles brought about through her intercession,[1] we will be touching on the role God is giving her to play in your hearts and the hearts of your children, and grandchildren, and great-grandchildren.

Why a story about a little Saint of Chastity? Why today? What does this mean to us, today? *What is chastity?*

Second Vatican Council II tells us:

"Especially in the heart of their own families, young people should be aptly and seasonably instructed about the dignity, duty, and expression of married love. Trained thus in this cultivation of chastity, they will be able at a suitable age to enter a marriage of their own after an honorable courtship." (GS 51)

---

[1] St. John Vianney, in particular, insisted that all credit for miracles people received at his church, be attributed to the intercession of St. Philomena

Above: *St. Philomena*

Above: *The Shrine of St. Philomena in Mugnano del Cardinale, Italy*

Right:
*St. John Vianney
The Cure of Ars
had a special devotion
to St. Philomena.
This statue of him is in
the Shrine of St.
Philomena in Mugnano
del Cardinale, Italy.*

If ever the world needed to know what chastity is, it is today. Let us try to explain the Church's teaching on chastity. *Exercising this noble virtue* (words almost forgotten which we must resurrect) *checks, controls, moderates, or excludes the desire and pleasure of carnal or sexual thoughts or actions. It is called the `angelic virtue' because the angels are pure by nature.*

There are two kinds of chastity: that which pertains to the *conjugal* love shared by married couples and *continence or purity* which is the chastity to be exercised by the young and unmarried people. Whereas with married couples, husbands and wives, chastity is the *control and moderation* of sexual relations, with youngsters and unmarried people it is the *exclusion* of sexual thoughts, desires or acts.

At one Papal audience, unaware the Pope was preparing the Catechism of the Catholic Church, we were amazed to hear Pope John Paul II say: *"If a man looks at his wife with lust in his heart, he is guilty of lustful thoughts and consequently of committing adultery."*[2] Was he not speaking, like St. Paul, before him, when he said that man must love his wife's body as his own? A month later, Pope John Paul II spoke of the responsibility of the media, to not entice married and unmarried alike into living a life of sin. And how did the media respond? You cannot put a secular program on T.V. most days without the subtle and not-so subtle suggestion to live lives of sin and perversion.

We wonder and are horrified that children are committing murders, often their own parents. I guess they figure *if Mommy could have killed me in her womb, its fair game that I can kill her. If it's all right to help someone commit suicide out of compassion, then I guess it's not murder if I help someone die.* Childish thoughts? Dear God, where are we going? Pope Paul VI said in *Humanae Vitae* if we use birth control, it will lead to

---

[2]Authors are paraphrasing his quotation

abortion which will lead to euthanasia and, we add, to shortening the life of those whose quality of life is not worth saving. Are we, like that monster Hitler thinking of a master race of clones?

Pope John Paul II speaks of the *"Culture of Death."* Sin is like locusts that swarm over a healthy field of flowers, devouring and then destroying all they cannot ravage. This chapter is for parents who have the responsibility and God-given right to save their children. These chapters are for the youth of the world. Look in the mirror Jesus holds up to you. Look at the faces of these young Saints. Look at the diabolical face of the devil. Whom do you choose?

Chastity is often confused as pertaining only to those taking a vow of celibacy or virginity. Although these vows include chastity, chastity can include these vows but not exclusively.

Chastity is to be exercised by all, in all walks of life. In a time of *decadence* - sexual permissiveness bringing on the murder of the innocents, *perversion* - its tentacles of self-hate gripping the souls of the young and innocent - through forced and enforced sex education beginning as early as the first grade,[3] same sex marriages - two daddys and two mommys, through schools and media of all kinds teaching homosexuality is the norm - loving, compassionate; and the cry for decency and following the Ten Commandments - unloving and archaic. Next, will they call God the Father, Jesus His Son and the Holy Spirit unloving and archaic? Oh, my God they already have and we have done nothing! And so, the enemy of God with his many disguises attacks the Holy Trinity.

---

[3]Read how sex education was instituted in the schools, by the masonic government of Mexico, beginning with the lowest grades, to tear down all family values, in an attempt to destroy the family unit and take control of the children, throw out the legitimate Roman Catholic Church and begin the destruction of the masses - all through sex education. For more on this, read Bob and Penny Lord's book: *Martyrs, they died for Christ.*

Is Saint Philomena a Saint?

When Saints like Saint Philomena were removed from the Church Calendar after Vatican Council II, many were hurt, thinking their favorite Saint had been deposed at best, and discredited at worst. I remember our son Richard Christopher (his baptismal name) being upset, when Saint Christopher was taken off the Calendar. Erroneously some said that it was because there was so little evidence these Saints had lived. Actually the telling and retelling of the stories of these Saints, down through the centuries, is reminiscent of the writers of the Old Testament.

With the Old Testament there is little *earthly remains* giving us clear evidence of the prophets' existence. We know of them solely through those who passed down their words and the events in their lives. Through this ongoing tradition, recalling the lives of the Prophets, one generation after the other heard the Word of God, their lives were influenced, and in turn the lives of the people of God to follow, down through the ages.

And what was God's plan? To teach, nourish, affirm and fortify generation after generation that there is a God and He has been faithful to them through thick and thin, in good times and bad, when they have been faithful and unfaithful, an unconditional loving Father Who never gave up on His conditional oftentimes unloving children.

But to alleviate any fears and correct any misconceptions, the Role Call of Pontiffs, beginning with Pope Gregory XVI, then Leo XII, Pius IX, Leo XIII, Pius X, and Benedict XV, using the supreme authority passed down to them from Jesus,[4] have

---

[4]Jesus made four promises to Peter in Matthew 16:16-18

(1) *"And I say to thee: that thou art Peter and upon this rock I will build My Church."* (2) *"The gates of hell shall not prevail against it."* (3) *"And I will give thee the keys of the Kingdom of Heaven."* (4) *"And whatsoever thou shall bind on earth, it shall be bound in Heaven; and whatsoever thou shall loose on earth shall be loosed in Heaven."* from *Treasures of the Church* by Bob and Penny Lord

declared, down through the centuries: Philomena a *Saint, Virgin and Martyr*.

This is my land; this is your land; this is our land

Since 1976, we have been going to Italy and Rome at least once and at most four times each year. Our first glimpse of the cupola of St. Peter's Basilica, looming over the trees of the Papal Gardens, never ceases to bring tears to our eyes; we are Home! This is our country, our Catholic country! Here brothers and sisters of different nations, cultures, color and creeds gather at the Home of the Apostles, that unbroken succession of Vicars of Christ, beginning with Peter. There are no divisions, no differences; we are one under the banner of the Keys of Peter.

Looking above, at the front of St. Peter's, you cannot help swallowing hard, to keep from bawling; your eyes go from Jesus in the middle, to the Apostles who are flanking Him on both sides. All you can think is, *No one on earth but we Catholics can boast this heritage, 2000 years of unbroken succession!* You hear the words in Church, *We are the Church founded by Jesus Christ, on the Rock of Peter*, but it is not till you come face to face with the reality, you look at St. Peter's Basilica, standing regally in the center of Vatican City, and then *"This is my Church, the Church which flowed from the Heart of Jesus on the Cross,"* are no longer words, but life! The words suddenly have flesh and bones, those of the living who come here to worship and pay respect to Jesus Christ and all His Popes, starting with St. Peter His first Pope, and of the dead who died loving and living for the Church, we too often take for granted.

You stand in the middle of the piazza of St. Peter's; you look about and think, this is my true home on earth. Here in the midst of pagan Rome majestically sits the capitol of the universal nation of over one billion faithful who call her their earthly home; she is the Vatican, and she is awesome!

This is holy ground; we are standing on holy ground.

Each pilgrimage, after we visit St. Peter's and pray before the tombs of the Popes who, with unbroken succession, succeeded our first Pope, we have the gift on Sunday, to be blessed by our dear Pope John Paul II at twelve noon, after we all recite the Angelus, together. Our hearts fill to overflowing, afraid they will burst with joy, we leave St. Peter's and go on to visit the other main Basilicas, St. John Lateran, St. Mary Major, and St. Paul outside the Walls.

This is always the *glorious*, seeing the magnificent tributes to Jesus and Mary in the ancient basilicas which the faithful had erected, over the years, in thanksgiving. Then we know that what awaits us is the price, the ultimate price paid so we could be Catholic. As we drive toward the Colosseum and the Circus Maximus, I think, Well, we have been on Mount Tabor and witnessed the Transfiguration; now it is time for the Way of the Cross that leads to Calvary. We walk slowly to the Colosseum. Entering, we look across the arena at the caves from which the Christians entered, thousands upon thousands of them, welcoming a torturous death rather than worship pagan gods. Across from those caves loom the caves from which the enforcers of their martyrdom, the ferocious lions would exit. We want like, St. Thérèse the Little Flower to kiss the ground, this holy ground, this ground drenched with the blood of Martyrs. But unlike St. Thérèse, we just stand there and weep.

The Catacombs - hallowed land of the living and the dead

Before we begin the heroic story of this young early Christian Martyr, it is necessary to tell you a little about where she was found - the Catacombs! From the Colosseum, the next stop for a pilgrim must be to the places, the holy places where the early Christian Martyrs, for the first three hundred years were brought, to be buried and remembered - the Catacombs.

If you listen to the wrong guide[5] in Rome, you will hear

---

[5]Guides in Rome are licensed by the Italian government

Above: *St. Philomena with arrows*
lilies, and anchor
Symbols she was a
Virgin and Martyr

Above: *Altar inside St. Philomena*
Shrine in Mugnano del Cardinale

Above: *Martyrdom of St. Philomena*

Above:
St. Philomena in Glory

what the different masonic governments, ruling Italy from time to time, have dictated be taught, that no Christians were martyred in the Colosseum. Then I have need to ask, *Why* did St. Thérèse kiss the ground; and *why* is there a cross standing on one side of the arena; and *why* does the Pope walk the Way of the Cross, processing around the Colosseum, on Good Friday, each year, and has done so, for two thousand years?

Then if you are so unfortunate, as to have the same guide or his/her clone, you will hear them say that the pagan Romans knew the Christians were down below in the Catacombs and that they knew they were burying their dead down there, and they left them alone. That's a nice fairy tale written by a few masons, but as far from the truth as they are Christians and they love Christ.

The truth is that the Catacombs were underground, hidden passages, in the vicinity of the Vatican. Here Popes, Bishops, Priests, brave and dauntless Martyrs, young and old alike, rich and poor, those of royal estate kneeling beside serfs, princes and paupers, all brothers, all Christians who loved Jesus, worshiped here on the tombs of the Martyrs. All partaking of the One Body, Blood, Soul and Divinity of Christ, the Eucharist, they did so knowing that some day their tombs would serve as altars for other Christians. For you see, in the early Church, Christians like St. Philomena knew to be a Christian was to surely die a Martyr's death. And they said Yes! When I think of all the poor, uninformed who do not believe in the Real Presence of Jesus in the Eucharist and in His Church, I want to ask them, if these Martyrs chose horrible deaths rather than deny He Who founded the Roman Catholic Church, how can they not belong to that Church which was bought by the precious Blood of the Lamb, and how can they not believe that He is alive and in our Church? Did they die for a piece of bread?

After the pagan sport and festivities, watching lions rip apart and mangle the precious bodies of Christians, were finally, mercifully over, the surviving Christians were allowed to take the remains of their loved ones to be buried. They chose the underground Catacombs, as they could be assured the bodies would not be desecrated there. Most pagans would not venture down into the Catacombs, because you could easily get lost in the maze of winding paths that made up this underground cemetery.

The persecution of Christians began in Nero's time, from 54-68 A.D. There is clear evidence of the existence of Catacombs from as early as 96 A.D. during the reign of the monster Domitian. The Catacombs are enormous and extend beneath much of Rome. It has been reported that over six million Christians were buried inside crypts fashioned by burrowing out soft rock from the Catacombs' surrounding walls. You can see these crypts, all sizes and shapes lining the long corridors, till today. The history of the early Church can also be found through the graffiti on the walls. This is how they discovered the relics of Saint Philomena.

The Church and her members survived *ten* bloody persecutions, with emperor after emperor, afraid of the power of Love, waging all-out war against helpless Christians. Rome, although possessing over sixty Catacombs, is not the only area where Catacombs can be found. They can be found in other parts of Italy.[6] We have seen them in Sicily; they can be found in France, Greece, parts of Africa, and Asia Minor.

When Constantine became a Christian, peace came to the Christians, our Church became legal, and the persecution stopped, for awhile. There was no need for underground Catacombs, except for pilgrims to come and venerate the relics of the Martyrs, and remember, remember the price paid for our Church!

But peace was not to last for our Church; her 2000 year history is filled with persecution from within as well as without,

---

[6]One of the best we have seen is in Bolsena, where the Miracle of the Eucharist, which brought about the Feast of Corpus Christi occurred; this is where the relics of another Virgin-Martyr were found, those of St. Christina.

with the Martyrdom of those who have always loved our Church lining the annals of our history. We are legitimate; time for another attack. The Church was in turmoil from within, with heresies cropping up, dissension threatening to destroy the Ship of our Church;[7] but this was an attack from without - the Lombards and the Goths invaded Rome! Believing the Catacombs contained priceless treasure (which it did, but not what they were seeking), they ransacked the tombs of the Martyrs. Not finding the treasures they were seeking, they spilled the dust of our beloved Martyrs onto the ground. That our hallowed relics would not ever be desecrated in the future, the Church transferred the remaining relics to churches around Rome. God always in charge, now they became accessible to all the faithful.

The Catacombs were pretty much abandoned until 1578, when the Holy See ordered they be opened and an investigation be made into any possible relics which might still be there. Over the years, our Popes commissioned qualified custodians to guard the treasures below - our Martyrs. When they discovered the remains of one of our Holy Ones, they would drop on their knees and pray; then they would carefully document their findings.

Such were the happenings on May 24, 1802, when archaeologists were once again digging in the Catacombs, and discovered a priceless treasure!

St. Philomena is discovered

Now it is important, we set the stage for this discovery. The world and the Church were in dire straits; it was time for God! The world looked like it was destined to be under the total domination of a new conqueror - Napoleon! He had ransacked churches, even placed his horses in the Basilica of St. Francis in Assisi. It looked dark for the Church, what did God do? God raised up a gentle but strong Pope - Pius VII. Napoleon, feeling

---

[7]Read Bob and Penny Lord's book: *Scandal of the Cross and Its Triumph, heresies throughout the history of the Church.*

omnipotent and puffed up by his importance, raised his heel against the Pope. The Pope, seeing the complacency and apathy of Nineteenth Century Europe, the hopeless resignation to slavery under Napoleon, decided only a renewal would halt the ever-moving onslaught of terror. It was time to change men's hearts!

But how? Go back to our roots, to the time of Christians ready to die for their Faith; go to the Catacombs. Guided by the Holy Spirit, the Pope commissioned archaeologists to make some digs in the Catacombs of Rome.

A light shines in the darkness!

What day should Jesus choose to help His vicar on earth? The Feast Day of *Our Lady Help of Christians!* May 24th, 1802, the remains of an early Christian Virgin-Martyr were unearthed! Archaeologists were digging in the Catacombs of the family Priscilla,[8] when they discovered a tomb which obviously had not been disturbed from the time the body of the Martyr had been entombed there. Carefully excavating the enclosure, they discovered the walls lined with red tiles (symbolizing a Martyr was buried there) with the Latin wording:

LUMENA - PAX TE - CUM FI

In the rush of closing the crypt, out of fear they would be discovered, the early Christians must have erred when they positioned the tiles; they did not make any sense! But in repositioning them, they discovered that they read:

PAX TE - CUM - FI - LUMENA

PEACE BE WITH YOU, PHILOMENA

When they opened the crypt area, they discovered not only the red tiles signifying a Martyr was buried there, but a rare sarcophagus of marble. As this was used only to bury a prominent member of the nobility or a Martyr, there was much excitement! The fact that she had been interred in the cemetery of Priscilla, Aquila's wife, contemporary of the Apostles and

---

[8]This catacomb is located under the road that leads out of Rome in the direction of Ancona, called the *Via Salaria*.

close friend of St. Paul, further affirmed this. They stopped excavating, and informed the Guardian of the Catacomb, who immediately ordered the area sealed.

The next day, when the tomb area was opened, they discovered symbols indicating a Virgin-Martyr. The burial stones surrounding the sarcophagus, bore several signs which clearly pointed to the Virginity and Martyrdom of the deceased person within! There was a lily signifying a *Virgin*; there were two arrows, one pointing upward and the other downward, conveying she had been pierced with arrows; there was an anchor suggesting she had been tied to an anchor and thrown into the river, there was a lance, signifying a means of Martyrdom.

Through the symbols and tiles, it is plain to see the Hand of God pointing to the relationship of the anchor with the Church, the anchor always having been a symbol of the Cross. *The Church and world was suffering; it was time for a Saint and Martyr to be discovered!* Is this why Philomena is coming to you, today? Have you been digging for some truth in your life?

There is not much written in the annals of the Church about this Virgin-Martyr whose name was obviously Philomena or in Latin *Filumena*, therefore the symbols were the only clue to who she may have been and what had happened to her.

When they opened the tomb, they found the relics of the Saint and a glass vessel containing dry blood, by her head.[9] As with other finds, the relics and the blood were tested. It is said that these relics gave clearer evidence of who and how this Martyr died, than when archaeologists have examined any of the other Martyrs interred in the Catacombs. The relics and blood were carefully placed in a wooden box, and then later investigated.

They discovered that the skeleton was that of a slight girl with small bones, all intact with not a bone broken. Scientists were able to discern that the skull had been fractured, the bones

---

[9]As this was the custom, placing a Martyr's blood near his/her body in the tomb, it was another indicator she had been a Martyr.

ordained and the Pope who was going to ordain him had a mutual
friend, King Ferdinand of Naples. Although this would not have
influenced the Pope in so serious a matter, it gave Don
Bartolomeo an opportunity to spend quality time with Pope Pius
VII and to confide the young priest's struggles and aims for his
parish in spite of his problems. Around the middle of May, Don
Bartolomeo asked his friend and secretary to accompany him to
the Treasury of the Relics.

Young Father Francesco di Lucia was shown relics after
relics; the last one was the one which grasped his heart -
Philomena! Her youth, her dedication to her vocation, her
willingness to lose all the world's treasures for the promised one
in Heaven was what the young of his parish needed - a romantic
role model, someone they could emulate, someone they could
look up to! Father Francesco wrote:

*"Upon seeing the vase containing her blood, which
preached a silent sermon to her courage, her sacrifice, and her
triumph, my determination overpowered me. At the same time I
realized that it would be utterly impossible for me, a poor priest
to be so favored, since the recognized relics of Martyrs are so
rare."*[12]

The little priest tried to hide the deep emotions this *little
Saint* had aroused in him; she had healed the wounds of disbelief
and strengthened him to forge on, no matter what others said.
But he could not share these feelings with his friend. He went
back to his room and shared them instead with his Best Friend -
Jesus. He prayed for God's Will, also praying that possibly it
could be the transfer of the relics to his little parish church. Even
as he prayed, he knew his petitions were impossible; only a
Bishop with the purpose of placing the relics in a cathedral could
hope to obtain them.

The custodian said, *first* of all, the relics had only been
discovered three short years ago; they needed to be safeguarded

---

[12]p.18 *St. Philomena, Powerful with God*, by Sr. Marie Helene Mohr, S.C. -
Tan Publishers

in the Treasury, in case there are any further findings; *secondly* they were too precious, as relics of Martyrs were rare, to be entrusted to a tiny, remote parish. Although the young priest appreciated the scruples and wisdom of the custodian, he was none-the-less heartbroken. But he decided to settle for any relic that would be available to him and his church.

The young canon of the Treasury gave him his own relic of a girl Saint, St. Ferma. No sooner had he brought the relic back to the residence where he and Don Bartolomeo were staying, then what should miraculously arrive - an ebony chest containing the relics of St. Philomena! The young priest now refused the relic, insisting it belonged in a more important church where the faithful could come and venerate.

Bishop-elect Don Bartolomeo ordered Father Francesco to keep the relic in his room for safekeeping. Word got out and priests began pouring in to see and venerate the little Martyr, Philomena. One night Father had an inner locution, a voice pleading with him to accept the offer made by the bishop and take her relics to his church in Mugnano del Cardinale. Father Francesco had contracted a high fever which had completely debilitated him. He prayed, if it were really Philomena who was speaking to his heart, then ask the Lord to heal him, at once! He was immediately healed, his fever gone and his strength renewed. The sacred relics were to be transported by the bishop and Father Francesco to Mugnano del Cardinale where they would be placed in the parish church of Father Francesco, Our Lady of Grace.

After Don Bartolomeo was ordained bishop, he and Father Francesco di Lucia entered the carriage which was to bring them to Mugnano del Cardinale. But when he sat down, the Bishop felt something pushing his legs from behind. He got up and looked; he could see nothing. The coachman, believing it was possibly the strong box on the floor, strapped it even more securely! The bishop returned to the carriage, and a second time he felt something strike his legs. He stepped down from the carriage, the coachman wedged the case even more than before, insisting after much apologies that the matter was settled; there was no way that case could move! The third time was too much for the bishop and he insisted everything be taken from the carriage so that they could discover the problem. Having done so, the last case removed, to their deep consternation, what did the poor clergymen see but that the precious ebony case, containing the relics of St. Philomena, had been placed on the floor! The coachman begged their forgiveness, saying since they had told him to take extra care with the ebony case, he jammed it in back of the other cases, so that there would no chance it would move and get damaged.

Needless to say, the rest of the journey, the ebony box was atop the seat facing the bishop and the two clergymen stayed praying on their knees in front of the relics of St. Philomena until it arrived in Mugnano del Cardinale, where it would to be later interred in Father's parish church.

Everywhere they stopped, miracles came about. In one village, they stopped at the house of a family where the mother had been terminally ill for a long time, and now she was dying. In spite of her illness, she sewed the most regal robes for St. Philomena's statue. The Bishop had authorized a papier-mâché image of St. Philomena to be made. The relics of St. Philomena had been unwrapped; the skull was covered by wax and a face was painted on the head of the statue; the bones were wired together and covered with wax. The only sad thing was that it did not really portray the loveliness of the Virgin-Martyr. But just one of the miracles which began immediately - as Donna Angela Rose was fitting the statue and sewing her outfit, the face of the statue kept changing expressions and emitting the most delightful perfume-like fragrances. She dressed the image, and Father Francesco and the bishop placed it in a lined box. The sadness which filled the house and the little village soon turned to joy - the woman of the house who had been so unconditionally generous had been healed!

There are so many miracles, a book could be written just

containing miracles coming to pass through the Virgin-Martyr's intercession. They are surely too numerous to share in this chapter. So many occurred, so quickly, one upon another that Father had to build a special chapel to St. Philomena. Her relics were placed inside the statue of St. Philomena that they'd had sculpted. After the new altar was completed, a screen was placed in front of the statue containing the blood of St. Philomena, only to be set aside when there was to be solemn exposition of the Saint for the faithful to venerate. On St. Michael's Feast Day, in 1805, when Father di Lucia slid away the screen, the statue had shifted, the Saint was lying on her side, her arm thrust out by her side holding two arrows in her hand; the arrows which had been previously pointing toward her heart were now pointing toward her feet. Her mouth was open delicately showing her teeth. Now, neither Father nor any of the parishioners had been satisfied with the way the statue had come out; but now, looking at St. Philomena's image, her coloring had changed, and she was beautiful.

The blind were made to see, the cripple to walk, no petition too small or too big, the little Saint had a lot of work to do. Word and evidence of miracles spread not only to the far reaches of Italy but into France. One of the most famous was that of Venerable Pauline Marie Jaricot.

The Miracle which shook the world

The world owes a debt to Venerable Pauline Marie Jaricot, for the founding of the Society of the Propagation of the Faith. But let us show you how God weaves the precious garment He has in mind for those who love Him. The home of the Jaricot family was always open to strangers journeying through Lyon. One day they had a visitor to whom they showed their usual generous hospitality. Père de Maggalon, of the Brothers of St. John of God showed his appreciation by giving them a gift of a tiny sliver of bone from the body of St. Philomena. Pauline humbly accepted the relic.

Now, Pauline knew of our little Saint because she had

heard the Curé of Ars[13] speak of her. Although, the little Saint had become very popular in Italy, because of the multitude of miracles brought about through her intercession, in France she was virtually unknown. But the Saint would touch Pauline and she, with the Curé of Ars, would make her well-known and revered by the French (and then the world) as she was with the Italians, as St. Philomena the *Miracle Worker.* The Curé asked Pauline for a relic of St. Philomena, in 1819, sixteen years before she was canonized!

By 1835, Pauline Marie Jaricot and the Curé of Ars had made St. Philomena a household word: *When in need of a miracle, pray to St. Philomena.* All the miracles that occurred in Ars, St. John Vianney always said, *"I can do nothing. It was St. Philomena!"* But one day, it looked as if one of St. Philomena's champions was going to die! Pauline was terminally ill with a failing heart condition. Her friend Père de Maggalon told her to go to Mugnano del Cardinale and ask St. Philomena for her intervention.

Pauline's doctor at first refused to hear anything of this ridiculous suggestion; she would not get far when she would have to turn back! But she was so insistent, he gave in and said yes; rather than an approval, it was more like granting her a last dying wish. Pauline left Lyon, with Mugnano del Cardinale in her sights. But first she would stop in Loreto and visit the Holy House where the Holy Family lived for most of Jesus' thirty-three years on earth. And then she would go on to Rome where she would ask for the Pope's blessing.

After traveling several weeks, she finally arrived in Rome. But sadly, she now had no strength left; she was almost dead; she had to pass on the audience with the Pope. Faithful and loyal daughter, unrelenting servant of Mother Church, Pope Gregory XVI determined if she could not come to him, he would go to her. Propped up, near death, she was speaking to the Pope of her

---

[13]another title for St. John Vianney

plan to combine the Society of the Rosary with the Society of the Propagation of the Faith.[14] The Pope, seeing she was dying, asked her to pray for him when she was in Heaven. She in turn asked him to pray for her to complete her trip to Mugnano del Cardinale. Then she said, if she were to return from Mugnano del Cardinale fully healed, would he speed up the cause of Philomena? He replied he would gladly do that, as that would be *"a miracle of the first order."*

When she finally arrived in Mugnano del Cardinale, the villagers were dismayed, seeing how close to death she was. This delicate little believer, frail in body but strong in faith, had traveled over the Alps, from one side of Italy to the other, from the north to the south through all kinds of obstacles, surely their Saint would honor so brave a soul. They gently carried her on a litter, into the church. They propped her up on the chair she had brought with her. Then with all the boldness of the people of southern Italy, they began entreating their Saint,

"Do you hear us, Philomena? If you do not cure this pious lady, we will pray to you no more! We will have nothing more to do with you! Please ask God to give you power to restore her to health right now! Yes, we shall keep our word!"[15]

All the villagers filled the church, praying for their adopted sister Pauline. She did not seem to be responding. Were they not shouting loud enough for their Saint to hear them, or was she upset with them for threatening her. Like Abraham before them, they pleaded, they bargained, and then they prayed!

August 10th, Pauline was in church; the priest raised the monstrance with our Lord Jesus enthroned within, and Pauline endeavored to kneel. Instead, she collapsed. She experienced a sensation unlike anything she had ever felt. Thinking she was dying, her nurse attempted to carry her out. Pauline waved to her nurse, to let her stay; she wanted her last moments and the last

---

[14]two Societies Pauline Marie Jaricot founded
[15]p.53 *St. Philomena, Powerful with God*, by Sr. Marie Helene Mohr, S.C. - Tan Publishers

things she saw on earth to be of this shrine. Everyone in the church was weeping; their Saint had let them down! Pauline's eyes were no longer on things of this earth; she was going Home!

Tears began to trickle down Pauline's face; color was coming back to her pale cheeks; she could feel a warmth filling her ice cold body, her hands began to feel life in them; a peace came over her. She became so serene, everyone wept all the more, sure she was leaving them!

She was afraid to let the others in the church know what she now knew, that she had been cured! As she was still weak, and fearing the excitement and passionate demonstration from the people when they discovered she was healed, she decided to allow her nurse to carry her out. But the following evening, when everyone saw her walking, they all rejoiced, for suddenly they all knew what she knew, St. Philomena had come through; she was healed! Pauline left her chair in the chapel as an *ex-voto* attesting to her miraculous cure!

Father de Lucia gave Pauline another relic of St. Philomena, which she had placed inside a statue of St. Philomena. They then carried the statue on the same litter which had carried Pauline into the Church, almost dead, days before. The villagers were processing the statue of the one whose intercession brought new life to Pauline, and Pauline, in turn, would spend the rest of her life promoting veneration to that little Saint, Virgin and Martyr.

Next stop Rome! Pauline walked into the audience chamber of the Vatican; she knelt before the Pope, and then, not recognizing the strong, well woman before him, he asked her to rise. Upon seeing her standing, Pope Gregory XVI was frozen. Then his amazement turned into awe and he asked,

"Is this really my dear daughter? And has she come back from the grave, or has God manifested in her favor the power of the Virgin-Martyr?"

Upon responding that it was indeed she who was standing before him, she went on to remind him of the promise he made to her before she left for Mugnano del Cardinale. The Pope asked her to remain in Rome for a year so that her cure could be authenticated, and she agreed. Her cure was declared a bonafide miracle and as a result, all the bishops unanimously declared Philomena a Saint.

Pope Gregory XVI asked the Sacred Congregation of Rites if a Decree should be issued allowing the faithful to pray to St. Philomena, and the answer was Yes! A Decree, granting the clergy permission to celebrate Mass in her name was issued by Pope Gregory XVI on January 30, 1837. In March, of the same year he proclaimed her worthy of her own Feast Day. St. Philomena is the only Saint from the Catacombs, of whom nothing was known except her name and the fact that she was a Martyr, who has been so honored.

The Curé of Ars and his Miracle Worker, St. Philomena

Pauline Marie Jaricot returned to Lyon, France and immediately went to Ars to visit her dear friend St. John Vianney. She related all the happenings surrounding her miraculous cure and gave the Curé a piece of the relic of St. Philomena. As Pauline spoke of St. Philomena, and how powerfully the little Virgin-Martyr had interceded for her in Mugnano del Cardinale, joy began to so fill the Curé's heart, he felt surely it would explode out of love for her. Tears came to his eyes; the little Saint had won another champion; he would advance devotion to her.

The Curé immediately had a chapel built for St. Philomena. Soon miraculous conversions, cures and return to the Sacraments began to occur, through Philomena and her little priest troubadour. She spoke to him, appeared to him, granted him his petitions; she became his *Heavenly Patroness*. As we have always said, the true sign of Sainthood and authenticity is *humility*. As the Curé was the personification of humility, his Way of the Cross was when miracles came about at his parish church in Ars. He would complain he wished St. Philomena would wait and allow the miracles to happen *away, far away* from him and his church.

We find ourselves writing about this Saint, our St. John Vianney, over and over again! Is it because God wants to remind His sons, His parish priests, those who have been ordained to be *"in persona Christi"*[16] that they are other Christs (*alter Christus*) and since Christ was the epitome of humility and holiness, He is speaking to them through their Patron Saint, St. John Vianney, to be holy and humble. Like John the Baptist, St. John Vianney wished to decrease so that the Lord and his Heavenly intercessor St. Philomena would increase.

Whether he wished it or not, miracles kept happening. As his heart was bigger than his body, he could not resist anyone asking for prayers. He prayed; then asked them to go pray to St. Philomena; and without fail, miracles came about, thousands of miracles. When you visit Ars, there is still some evidence of the favors asked for and received.

The Curé had always been frail and fragile, but the time came when it looked like he had no more to give. Each day he grew weaker and weaker.   His usual practice of spending anywhere from sixteen to eighteen hours in the confessional, and then mounting the pulpit to deliver a sermon became more and more impossible, until one day he had to stop in the middle of his homily and be assisted off the pulpit.   Each day what little strength he had, ebbed out of his body, lowering and lowering his resistance, debilitating him so, he was not only helpless to fight the illness, the illness was robbing him of one loving faculty of his priesthood after the other.   Finally he could no longer rise from his modest bed. A doctor was called in and he reported the prognosis was grave - the Curé was dying! His confessor gave him the Last Rites of the Church, the Sacrament of Extreme Unction.

St. John Vianney asked that Mass be celebrated at the altar of St. Philomena, and that he be present. They helped him into

---

[16]in the person of Christ

the chapel. Suddenly he began to tremble uncontrollably: he became agitated; one could smell the fear of death in the church. His nurse who loved him dearly, tried to hold back the tears; he was dying! But the moment the Mass commenced at the Altar of St. Philomena, a peace came over the little priest; his countenance changed; rather he looked as if he had seen something; or was it someone? When the Mass ended, he told them he had been cured! The nurse later reported hearing him speak to someone, uttering the name *Philomena!*

When others saw what had happened, they exclaimed it was a miracle! He replied they were right, it was nothing short of a Miracle! He had no problem identifying the means God took to spare him, so that he could continue serving Him on earth a little while longer; he gave all credit to the intercession of, you guessed it, St. Philomena! As soon as he recovered sufficiently, he went to his beloved Philomena's altar and prayed in thanksgiving. And then, as he and we know no one, not even the Blessed Mother no less St. Philomena, can bring about a Miracle without the Will of the Lord, the Curé prostrated himself before His Lord so Real and Present in the Blessed Sacrament on the Altar. When he had been at the point of death, before his miraculous healing, *the Little Saint* had revealed things to him, both sad and glad which he would remember to his dying hours.

We thought we had written all there was to write on the Curé in our book on men Saints,[17] but as we wrote on mystics and other subjects concerning the Church and her history, we found him entwined and intermeshed in the fabric which makes up the Roman Catholic Church and all her treasures!

St. Philomena makes herself known!

What do we know about St. Philomena? It is August, 1833, and we find Mother Mary Luisa, Superior General of the

---

[17]Bob and Penny Lord's book: *Saints and other Powerful Men in the Church*

Congregation of the Dolours of Mary,[18] praying before the statue of St. Philomena. The discovery of St. Philomena's relics, thirty-one years before, and the miracles attributed to her intercession had made the Virgin-Martyr well known, throughout Italy. Because of her instantaneous response to prayers and petitions, she had earned the title: *Miracle Worker.* Although Mother Mary Luisa believed in the veracity of the relics and the authenticity of the Saint found in the Catacombs of Priscilla, she could not help questioning, trying to probe into what may have happened to have made this young Virgin a Martyr.

Try as she may, to keep her mind on her meditations, her thoughts would wander to the underground crypt and St. Philomena. As she was contemplating what may have happened, a thought came to her; it was as if the little Saint was speaking to her. The voice introduced herself as Philomena,[19] the daughter of a Grecian King and Queen who ruled over a small Greek principality. She went on to tell Mother Mary Luisa that as her parents had not been converted to the One True God, and were childless, they prayed and offered sacrifice to pagan gods.

There was a doctor from Rome, named Plubius who was physician for the royal family. As he lived in the palace, he grew very close to the King and Queen, and became aware of their distress, at not having any children. One day, filled with the Holy Spirit Who alone can convert, he spoke to them of the one True God and the miracles that He had brought about, out of love for His children. He promised he would pray for their intentions, if they would consent to be baptized and convert to Christianity. He spoke so powerfully, the Holy Spirit using him, their minds were open and their hearts turned to the Lord; they consented to be baptized; they converted to Christianity and their heart's desire was granted; a child would be born!

A precious baby girl was born; she was so delightful, her

---

[18]She died in the odor of Sanctity in the year 1875. (p.87 *St. Philomena, The Wonder Worker* by Father Paul O'Sullivan, O.P. - Tan Publishers
[19]You recall that the tablets in the Catacombs spelled out Philomena.

parents fawned over her. Her baby sounds, so long desired, now resounded throughout the palace, lifting their spirits; sunshine flowed into the once dismal rooms, showering a bright light onto their gray stone walls. The little baby immediately filled the palace with joy. Because she had brought light into their lives, through *the Light* - Our Lord Jesus,[20] they named her *Lumena*. This also symbolized the light of Faith that she had brought into their lives! They would change her name to *Filumena*, the day they had her baptized. Filumena said they named her *Filumena* which means *daughter of light*, because on that day through baptism, she was a new creation, born anew to the Faith her parents had adopted. We can see the seed of faith planted in this dear couple, growing.

As Filumena (or Philomena) grew in holiness, she also grew in loveliness. She was the apple of her parents' eyes and hearts. They took her with them, everywhere they went. This would prove to be disastrous! Diocletian, the wicked Emperor of Rome was threatening to attack their small state. Their only hope was to go to Rome. Her parents felt, if they appealed to him, they might be able to avert a war they could not possibly expect to win. As they could not bear to leave her, they brought Filumena with them to visit the Emperor. That was a monumental mistake!

Filumena was thirteen years old, and she had blossomed into a breathtakingly beautiful young girl. As soon as the little family entered the reception hall, and Diocletian spotted Filumena, his eyes never left her. Her father pleaded with him to not invade their tiny principality, arguing it was of little consequence. Growing weary, the King felt all was lost, as the Emperor paid little or no attention to him or to what he was saying. Finally he ceased speaking; what more could he say!

Then Diocletian spoke. He told him to have no fear; not only would he not attack his domain, he would place his giant

---

[20]because out of their desire to have her, they had initially agreed to be baptized

army at the King's disposal; he would protect him and his kingdom from this day on. There was only one condition. With the devil there is always one condition, always a price to pay. The price the King and Queen would pay would be one beyond their darkest fear! Diocletian asked for only one thing - to marry their most precious daughter.

The awesome honor, he believed was being bestowed on them and Filumena, triumphed over his good judgment, her father agreed immediately. They left for their own palace. All the way home, her parents were planning, excitedly anticipating the upcoming royal marriage! All they could think was: *Their daughter was going to become an Empress!* Filumena's protests seemed to fall on deaf ears. They tried cajoling, then insisting they only wanted what was best for her. Filumena had always been an obedient daughter, but now *she* insisted she could not agree to this sinful union, as the Emperor was already married.

Once home, the arguing continued, Filumena crying, her parents reasoning; Filumena pleading, her parents unflinching. The more she protested, the more they tried to convince her this was a tremendous honor and opportunity - to be the spouse of an Emperor. But all the more, she protested she had promised her hand to the Omnipotent King of the Universe - her Lord Jesus; she had pledged her virginity to Him and it was no longer hers or theirs to dispose of as they willed.

She insisted that although she loved them dearly, she would not go back on her promise to her Lord. She tried to reason with them, pleading, *"Would you for the love of a man have me break my word to my Lord Jesus Christ?"* They countered with, *"You were too young to make such a decision."* Imploring turned into insisting, into threatening the most fearsome punishment, if she did not comply with her father's wishes. This was a side of him she had never seen; and though she was upset and frightened, with only the Grace that the Lord could give her, she stood firm!

Her father really loved her deeply. He tried to reason with

the Emperor, asking to be released from his promise, arguing the child is too young, give her time. Diocletian would not allow his desires to be circumvented. A promise had been made, and unless he wanted to suffer the circumstances....

Her mother who had been on the sidelines, joined in the fray. She sided in with Filumena's father. They employed every tactic. United, they tried coaxing, pleading; but all to no avail; finally losing patience, they tried wielding the most menacing threats. Filumena remained strong and resolute; but it was to get difficult, even for her. Her parents fell on their knees, before her, pleading for themselves, their country and their helpless subjects who would suffer if she persisted. Not many of us are made of the stuff of Saints and Martyrs. They have a Heavenly resolve and strength which surpasses all understanding. Filumena spoke gently but firmly to her dear parents. I wonder if her parents were thinking what parents often think, *When did she grow up; it was only yesterday we were welcoming her into this world!*

She turned to them: *"No,"* she insisted, *"My vow of virginity which I have promised to my Lord comes before everything, before parents, country, subjects. My kingdom is not of this world, but of Heaven."* Two scripture passages come to mind, the one where Jesus speaks of those who give up mother and father, and etc. for the Kingdom;[21] and when standing before Pilate, Jesus responds, *"My Kingdom is not of this world."*[22]

She could see her parents deeply wounded, and it in turn wounded her, but she could not place anyone before her Lord. And so, leaving no other recourse, they brought their precious daughter to the Emperor's chambers. Now Diocletian was not one to disobey; he tortured and killed others for less than what she was doing; but he was really attracted to this spotless virgin, and the more she resisted the more he wanted her. It became an obsession!

Often those who have every earthly possession, begin to

---

[21]Mk 10:29
[22]Jn 18:36

think they are gods, that they can do whatever they will and have whatever they desire. Not ever having been denied anything on earth, he was not going to allow a little slip of a girl to have that victory. He tried to win her with promises of splendid clothes, position and power, to array her with precious diamonds and gems. Furious, the devil within him exposed himself, taking over; the Emperor, having seen his sweet talk and vile threats fail, ordered Filumena thrown into the dungeon.

Her jailers took delight in demeaning the little princess, as they tightly wrapped heavy chains about her fragile body. Diocletian visited Filumena every day, hopeful that the physical suffering and the emotional pain (because of the disgrace being visited upon her family as well as herself) would sway her and she would give in to his lustful desires.

Hoping she had enough, after several days of endless torture, alone except for her foul-smelling vile jailer, Diocletian ordered her released from her chains that she might eat some bread and drink a bit of water. He had tried everything, bribing, threatening, now he attacked her purity, subjecting her virtuous soul to the most filthy language and innuendoes. This leading only to another defeat, he added new tortures to the almost unbearable ones she had previously suffered. She armed herself with the Armor of God,[23] her eyes and soul soaring upward toward her *Heavenly Home*, Jesus and Mary sustaining her. It reminds me of St. Patrick's prayer: *Christ with me; Christ in me; Christ before me, Christ behind me; Christ beneath me; Christ above me; Christ on my right hand; Christ on my left;...*

She had been languishing in her damp dreary cell for thirty-seven days, when our Blessed Mother appeared to her, a Heavenly light glowing around her. She was holding the Child Jesus in her arms. She told Filumena that she had three more days of this prison; then forty days of imprisonment having passed, she would be released from the never-ending pain she

---

[23]Eph 6:11

had endured for her Lord. In her humanness the thought of this torture finally at an end filled Filumena with new hope and courage. Seeing Mother Mary and the Child Jesus was to her, like the experience Peter, James and John had on Mount Tabor. Her Calvary was soon to come. Jesus and Mary had given her this glimpse of Heaven; it would fortify her for the days ahead.

Our Lady reminded her that when she was baptized, she had been named Lumena, meaning light. She told her to fear not, that she, Mother of *the Light*, Filumena's Spouse Jesus, would help her. The Blessed Mother told her that though her human strength betray her, Gabriel, the same Angel who never left *Her* side, would be beside Filumena; She, Mary his Queen, would recommend her to his care. She went on, assuring her that with Gabriel beside her to support her, Filumena would have the strength to withstand all the devil could throw at her. The vision left as quickly as it had appeared, leaving a Heavenly fragrance behind, an incense which rose to the Heavens; and with it Filumena's soul soared, as if on a perfumed chariot.

Blessed Mother's warning had not come too soon. The fortieth day came and with it Diocletian's uncontrollable wrath. As she would not succumb to torture, which made men a hundred times stronger surrender, he would publicly humiliate her. The ultimate shame: This body which she kept for her Lord, he would have stripped so that all could see her in her nakedness; and then, like that King Whom she preferred to him, she too would be scourged by order of *this Emperor* who ruled *this* world! He said:

"Since she is not ashamed to prefer, to an emperor like me, a malefactor condemned to an infamous death by His own people, she deserves that my justice shall treat her as He was treated."[24]

By the Grace of God, the guards did not choose to strip her of all her clothes, but scourged her partially clothed,

---

[24]p.124 *St. Philomena, Powerful with God,* by Sr. Marie Helene Mohr, S.C. - Tan Publishers

whipping her until her clothes were soaked red by her blood. Gabriel beside her, although she was suffering the most excruciating pain, she did not faint.

Diocletian had her dragged, a pitiful sight before all the high personages of the Court, to her cell to die! At last, she thought, I will be with my Savior. But it was not the end. God had need to use her, a little more. In her cell, a light cut through the darkness and with it two Angels appeared. They poured a sweet, cooling salve on her open gaping wounds and Filumena said it soothed her, making her feel better than before she had been scourged.

When the prison guards reported that she looked better than before her public scourging, Diocletian ordered her brought to him. Not discouraged by all the rejection, he was more insistent than ever. Upon seeing her apparent miraculous healing, Diocletian tried to convince Filumena that Jupiter and another god whom he had sent were responsible for this phenomenon. He tried to coerce her, saying that it was Jupiter's wish she become Diocletian's Empress. Now, what young girl would not give in to the attention being paid her, after all the Emperor said that Jupiter himself had chosen her to marry Diocletian! He tried softening her with promises of great position and power in the Court, and in the world. He began speaking to her, sweetly, trying to seduce her with words and then made so bold as to try to physically.

The Truth will always conquer the father of lies. So, with every enticement Diocletian offered Filumena, she counteracted with the Word of God which completely affirmed her belief in God and her desire to belong to Jesus, alone. Furious, he ordered an anchor be chained tightly around her neck, and she be thrown into the Tiber River. The Emperor's guards carried out his orders; Filumena was cast into the river, anchor and all, left to drown. But God sent two of His Heavenly Messengers to loosen the anchor from around her neck, freeing her to rise to the surface. The anchor stuck in the river mud where it has remained, for all time, in remembrance of God's power!

Now, what do you think happened? Right! Those waiting on the side of the river, upon seeing this miracle, followed Filumena, proclaiming their belief in her God and converted! Diocletian, blinded by fury fumed she had used black magic. Isn't it strange how the evil one continues to accuse the holy of that which he is guilty?

All right, he thought, *the anchor and the Tiber river did not kill her, I'll have her dragged through the streets of Rome, and have my best archers shoot arrows at her.* The little brave soldier of Christ bled, as she staggered through her torturous march. Although the pain became so severe she thought she would faint, she did not. Gabriel again sustained her, I'm sure. Seeing her more dead than alive, Diocletian had her removed to her cell, once again. I wonder? Was Filumena getting to the people, with her belief and her willingness to suffer any indignation for that belief?

Back in her cell, she fell into a deep sleep, the sleep of the Angels. She awakened refreshed, which only added fuel to the fire. Diocletian had her *again* paraded through the streets, archers shooting arrows at her, but it seems there was not enough force and they fell to the ground, without hitting their mark. Diocletian was present and saw what had come to pass. He called in a magician, who told him the only way to overcome this sorcery was with fire!

Diocletian smugly wondered what Filumena would do against heated arrows! He ordered them fired in a furnace until the spearheads of the arrows became broiling hot. The archers once again, bent their bows, arched them and let the red-hot arrows fly. They aimed for her heart; but the arrows boomeranged and instead of striking her, they struck the archers, killing *them*. The six who had aimed, died; the rest converted to Christianity and put down their bows and arrows.

It wasn't enough she had foiled death, the Emperor was losing his hold over his subjects. Seeing what had been transpiring, word got around speaking of God's power. The crowd began to cheer Filumena on! This further inflamed Diocletian; he ordered her beheaded! The little bird of Paradise, Filumena flew to her Spouse in Heaven. She told Sister Mary Louise that it was Friday, August the 10th, at three o'clock in the afternoon, when at last her spirit soared up to Heaven.

Coincidence? That the world would believe the account we just shared with you, the Lord willed that Filumena's body which had been retrieved from the Catacombs be brought to Mugnano del Cardinale on August 10th!

Other accounts came in and verified this account, and if that is not enough, the fruits speak for themselves. Thousands upon thousands of miracles have happened since that fateful day when Filumena's relics were found and unearthed from the Catacombs.

Do we believe that God sent this sign to us, this Filumena, a little light testifying with her martyred body, her belief in The Light?

"In the beginning was the Word, and the Word was with God; and the Word was God. He was in the beginning with God. All things were made through Him, and without Him was made nothing that has been made. In Him was life, and the life was the light of men. And the light shines in the darkness; and the darkness grasped it not."[25]

She believed John's words. And she died for them!

---

[25]John 1:1

St. Rose of Viterbo

This is the story of a Saint and a Sinner. This story, another part of our 2000 year journey as a Church and a people of God, is about *Rose* who was raised to Sainthood and *Frederick* the sinner who God would use to raise her to that height of piety and virtue which forms a Saint.

How did we get to know this virtually unknown Saint (in the United States)? In 1976 Bob and I made our first pilgrimage to Europe and the Holy Land. In 1977, Bob and I returned, only now with our ten year old grandson, Rob. We became the three musketeers, beginning an exciting quest, *our Journey of Faith to Jesus, Mary, the Angels and the Saints*. It was a great experience which brought us from Belgium, to France, to Italy that year. We were forty-two days on the road, going to the many different pilgrimage sights we had researched. It was a great adventure! Everyone thought we were crazy bringing a ten year old to Europe, in the first place; and then to compound it by traveling overseas for forty-two days was the crowning lunacy, they maintained. Well let me tell you, that ten year old was a better pilgrim at times, than we were.

What brought us to Rose of Viterbo, initially? She was a Saint whose body the Lord left incorrupt[1] on earth, as one of the signs of her sanctity. A body which has not decomposed, and is miraculously preserved, is *one*, only *one* of the signs which the Lord gives us to recognize someone's holiness; it is not what makes one a Saint. This particular sign is strictly a gift to the *Saint* verifying the Lord's miraculous intervention, and a gift to *us*

---

[1]An incorrupt body is one which has not decomposed, or suffered the decaying process which normally begins, at the moment of death. With Saints and Blesseds whose bodies have not decomposed, no preservative chemicals have been injected into their bodies, no embalming or mummification; nor have any chemicals been found which the bodies could have produced *naturally* to cause this preservation. In these cases, there has been no medical or scientific reason why the body has not decomposed.

Above:
St. Rose of Viterbo

Below:
St. Rose of Viterbo went among the villagers of Viterbo feeding their bodies and souls.

Right:
St. Rose of Viterbo converted a heretic by walking through fire.

Left:
St. Rose of Viterbo listens to a friar and is filled with the Holy Spirit.

of God's power and love; what will He not do to bring us closer to Him, through faith! Consequently, he leaves us signs, or gifts to help us in our journey toward Him and Heaven.

[Author's note: In the case of Padre Pio, for example, although he had all the gifts: bilocation, stigmata for forty years, perfect confessor, reading men's hearts, this is not what the Holy See has used to determine his (or anyone's) holiness in the Cause for Beatification and ultimate Canonization. Padre Pio has been judged,[2] as with all candidates, for the virtuous life he led in his vocation, in his case the priesthood.][3]

Once again, the world is in turmoil and the Church is under attack. *Without Compromise!* Our Lord Jesus would not compromise and they crucified Him. His loyal Vicars would not compromise, and they along with Mother Church, over our 2000 year history, have been nailed to the Cross! Knowing this, our Popes, His Vicars, chosen as they are by and through the intervention of the Holy Spirit, live and die for their spotless spouse, the Church.

A Sinner, a Saint, and a Pope without compromise

We are in the days of conquests and greed. Greed desiring more, requiring more; and then requiring more, conquering more. Out of necessity, to feed this giant, conquests begot conquests; and so the freedom St. Paul spoke of, we no longer slaves,[4] was once again set aside, the sacrifice of the many for the power of the few.

To set the stage, we will begin with the *sinner*, Frederick II, his grandfather Frederick I Barbarossa (a Roman Emperor dating back to the Twelfth Century), and his father Emperor

---

[2]Padre Pio was made Venerable and he will be beatified Spring of 1999. For more on Padre Pio, read Bob and Penny Lord's book: *Saints and other Powerful Men in the Church.*

[3]For more stories on other Saints who had the stigmata, fragrance of heaven, who bilocated, had visions, whose bodies were incorrupt, read Bob and Penny Lord's many books on the *Saints, Visionaries, Mystics and Stigmatists* listed at end of this book.

[4]Gal 4:7

Henry VI. As with all monsters, Hitler in the Twentieth Century and Frederick I, the Red Beard[5] in the Twelfth, we the foolish, believe we can coexist with them. So did the papacy in the Twelfth Century with Frederick I! We will show you how the Holy See again and again attempts to coexist with one after the other, first Frederick I, then Frederick I's son, Henry VI and his heir apparent Frederick II, who would follow in his grandfather's footsteps.

What began as cooperation between the Papacy and his grandfather Frederick I would turn into Frederick I's greed overcoming his good judgment, as he went about trying to reestablish the *Carolingian* rule of the Ninth Century and *the Ottonian* rule of the Tenth Century in Italy, which gave the Emperors the *royal right* to take over the Church and all the papal states, not only choosing prelates and making the bishopric a part of the Empire, but requiring all bishops be *friends* of the Emperor, taking all their orders from him.

[If you study the history of the Church,[6] you will see that the bear which seems to die in one century, will revive in another century with the same desires, the same heresies, the same attacks, and the same ferocity. Is this not what happened when the German princes were able to use Martin Luther to do their dirty work, separating the Church in Germany from the One True Church, the Roman Catholic Church, for the supreme purpose of confiscating papal lands donated to the Church over the centuries by grateful Kings and Queens!]

Jesus said, *"A house divided against itself will not stand."*[7] The northern states of Italy, tiny little fragmented states under separate rulers,[8] separated from each other and the other little kingdoms of Italy, were fair game for any conqueror desiring to

---

[5]Barbarossa in Italian means Red Beard
[6]Read Bob and Penny Lord's book: *Scandal of the Cross and Its Triumph, Heresies throughout the History of the Church.*
[7]Mt 12:25
[8]There were over 27 city states, prior to the unification of Italy.

plunder and vanquish the divided weak. Frederick I decided the way he could make Italy once again an Empire, a *Hohenstaufen Empire*, was to begin with the conquering of the northern states of Italy. But he did not count on the Lombard League who was in alliance with the Pope of that time, Alexander. Frederick I was defeated in Legnano. Reconciliation came about between the Pope and Frederick I, and consequently an alliance between Frederick and the northern states. Whereas in the Peace of Constance he granted the states some sort of *de facto* self-government, he maintained for himself and his heirs monumental rights as overlord.

"*To the victor goes the spoils,*" was no less true then than now! Although all his attempts at world domination were vanquished in his lifetime, Frederick I would be victorious in the end! What he could not do with force, he did using his well-known infamous maneuvering: he married his son Henry VI to the heiress of the Kingdom of Sicily.[9] In this way, he realized his dream to establish a *Hohenstaufen Empire* in Italy. As the empire now encircled the papal states, it not only weakened their position but it made the communes (northern states) vulnerable. Gregory VIII became Pope. Frederick I, seeing the world-wide domination, emanating from the onslaught of Saladin and his troops of Saracens, summoned his soldiers and headed the Third Crusade for the Holy Land. Even that was to be thwarted, as he drowned crossing the Saleph River in Asia Minor.

Upon his father's death, Henry VI was crowned King of Germany in 1169, King of Italy in 1189, and then King of Sicily in 1191; he was also crowned Emperor that year. Unlike his father, Henry was not very charismatic; he lacked his father's warmth, the charm that won so many over to his father. But what Henry lacked in personality, he surpassed his father in knowledge and love of the Catholic Faith, that which he probably received from his strong Catholic mother, Queen Beatrice. During his

---

[9]which at that time encompassed much of southern Italy

brief rule, he had three aims:

one to gain the approval of the German princes, as he came to the throne through hereditary succession, his father being from the Hohenstaufen family;

two to arrange an agreeable territorial agreement with the Papacy;

and *three* to lead a Crusade to the Holy Land, completing what his father had started - the deliverance of Jerusalem and all the Shrines of the Holy Land from the hands of the Saracens.

Poor Henry VI's *first aim* was to fail in that the German princes, while they did not hesitate to elect Henry's *infant* son King, they did reject the doctrine of automatic succession to the throne by virtue of royal birthright, in this case, the *Hohenstaufen* family. The *second aim* failed, as the new Pope Clement III was wary of dealing with Henry, who had too much power and was a decided threat to the Papacy, not only as King of Germany but through marriage,[10] as King of Sicily. His *third* aim to lead a Crusade to the Holy Land was blessed by the Pope; it received great acclaim by the German citizens, but alas it too was to fail; Henry died the night he was to leave for the Holy Land, resulting in his troops returning and abandoning the Crusades.

The Empire was divided between Henry's brother Philip of Swabia and his infant son Frederick II.

We have heard the age-old adage, *"Like father, like son,"* well maybe because of Henry VI's sudden death and division of the empire, great catastrophes were averted and he was not able to fulfill his father's dream, like conquerors before and after him, of world domination. But the adage would become a prophecy, only, *"Like grandfather, like grandson;"* for a second Frederick would rise from the ashes of his grandfather's failure and become a pawn for the greedy seeking that which is not theirs.

Before she died, His mother, the Empress entrusted Frederick II to Pope Innocent III. When Emperor Otto I (who

---

[10]His wife's father was Roger II, King of Sicily

had feigned loyalty to the Pope) turned against the Papacy, the Pope supported his loyal ward, Frederick II, to rule over Italy. Through this, Innocent III prevented Otto I from gaining supremacy over Italy and the confiscation of not only Italian principalities but papal lands, as well. Frederick II, was victorious blocking the takeover of Italy by Otto I.

When Frederick II took over principality after principality in Italy, it was without incident. He was welcomed not only by the Italians but Pope Honorius[11] who placed the Imperial crown on his head. At that time, Frederick II pledged his loyalty to the Cross and the Papacy. But things got strained between the Pope and Frederick II, as his ambitious appetites for more and more power, grew more and more ravenous. The renewed threats to the Papacy and the northern states resulted in doubt, disbelief, distrust, fear and ultimately bitterness. Frederick II, thirst for power never fully quenched, went about not only unifying Italy under himself (of course), but waging a campaign for her reentry into the Roman Empire, with him as Emperor.

His borders of influence dangerously kept expanding. The papal states, seeing the danger in the progressively unrestrained inordinate power Frederick was amassing, in the *world*, feared the Church would be next. Sure enough, in 1231 Frederick made unbridled demands on the northern part of Italy, including the confiscation of lands belonging to the Papacy. The new Pope Gregory IX *condemned* Frederick, accusing him of desecrating, looting and pillaging Church property and charged him with heresy! Frederick's ambition to found an Empire, on the strength of his takeover of all Italy, was forestalled by the Pope's action.

A rose will bloom in the desert

For the *second time* Frederick II was excommunicated; he retaliated by attacking the papal states, and this is where Rose of Viterbo came in. In 1240, Frederick II decided to occupy Viterbo! The Lord always with us, in time of need, sent into this

---

[11]who succeeded Innocent III

world of hopelessness and helplessness, a baby! A few years before the frightening entry of Frederick II into the sweet, serene village of Viterbo, there was an entry that would inflame the populace with new courage and hope, a child was born! Little Rose, who was named when she was baptized, would let out a cry that would grow and grow until it awakened the people to a new consciousness that they could make a difference.

Her parents were not of noble birth, but had instead the gifts needed by a future Saint, holiness, virtue, piety, humility and charity.   From her earliest years, Rose showed an alive, unending, overflowing love for the Church, for Jesus, the Blessed Mother, the Angels and the Saints.   When she was just eight years old, she had a vision of the Blessed Mother in which Mother Mary told Rose she would be clothed in the habit of St. Francis.[12] She was not to become a cloistered Nun, but a tertiary, part of the third order, remaining at home, giving witness to her family and neighbors by word and action of Jesus in her life.

She later became ill. But the Lord having too much for her to do, she soon recovered and donned the habit of the lay penitents of St. Francis. When she began, to contemplate Jesus' suffering, and how wounded He was by the ingratitude of His children, Rose went to the people of Viterbo, preaching in the streets, knocking on doors, going from house to house, berating her neighbors for their complacency and apathy toward the freedom they had lost at the hands of Frederick II.

She told them they could be free; all they had to do was overthrow the Ghibelline[13] garrison. *She was all of age twelve!* But her age did not deter the populace from listening, their hearts on fire! It had been so long since anyone had spoken of the beauty of Italy, of the promise the Lord made to His children not to leave them orphans. She told them they were not born to be slaves, but free!   They listened!   And miracles came about! Everywhere she went, she was greeted warmly; citizens having

---

[12]Now it was just about fifteen years since St. Francis had died.
[13]or *Hohenstaufen* barracks, soldiers under the command of Frederick II

heard of her and the marvels surrounding her speechmaking, gathered to hear the Good News! Men who no longer had the will to get up in the morning were plowing their land, once more; after all, it was their land, little Rose had said so. And so, new life came into the ancient village of Viterbo.

Crowds began to gather; her father became nervous; soon, the authorities would hear of her and they would all be punished. What was wrong with her; after all, they had food on their table! He scolded; he pleaded; he berated her; he cajoled her; finally, she leaving him no recourse, he threatened to beat her if she did not stay home and cease her preaching. Rose replied, *"If Jesus could be beaten for me, I can be beaten for Him. I do what He has told me to do, and I must not disobey Him."*

Father and daughter seemed at loggerheads, when the local parish priest intervened; he urged her father to cease restraining Rose from doing her Divinely appointed duty. He withdrew his objections and Rose was free to preach; and preach she did, tirelessly rising early in the morning, retiring late at night, as if one driven, knowing time was short. This sounds like the urgency Jesus had with three *short* years to reach the children of God. This sounds like the time of Jesus; it sounds like today, with the few speaking out, the John Baptists of our day crying out in the desert, *Repent and be saved!* And the many.....?

She was free to preach for two years! Standing on the street corners of the town, crowds gathering, clamoring for more, her voice crying out, theirs joining in, they were a people to be reckoned with, she was uniting them, rallying support for the Pope and the Church. They took up the cry, Defend the Pontiff's cause! *Then*, some villagers who had sold their souls to the Emperor for land and position became alarmed and began clamoring for her execution as an enemy of the Empire.

The mayor of the town would hear nothing of it, protesting the girl was innocent. He had a few reasons for his defense of Rose; he was a fair and just man, but also a prudent and wise man. He feared for his life, for by this time, Rose had become a little Joan of Arc. The townspeople had been resigned to the carnage of their existence; Rose brought them reason for hope and rejoicing. There was a light at the end of the dark tunnel they had been journeying through, and the mayor pitied anyone trying to put out that light.

What was the wisest course? Banish Rose and her parents from the village. And so he ordered them escorted out of town! The little family settled in Soriano; and it was there that Rose prophesied, announcing to all, the forthcoming death of Frederick II looming in the near future. He died in Apulia, on the thirteenth of that month. The papal party was reinstated in Viterbo; the citizens of Viterbo were slaves no more; free, at last.

Their little heroine was also now free, to return to her beloved village; but not before she was to go through a test by fire, truly fire! A citizen of Soriano, loyal to the Emperor and the royal Hohenstaufen family, threatened Rose with burning to death at the stake, if she did not renounce the Pope; Rose responded by asking her to be quick about it, thanking her for the privilege of dying a martyr's death for the Faith. Having completely confounded her adversary, she not only disarmed her, she won her over for Christ and His vicar, the Pope.

Rose returned to Viterbo with her parents. It was time to go to the Convent of *St. Mary of the Roses* in Viterbo and ask for entrance as a postulant. As her parents were not able to supply the necessary dowry, the abbess refused her entry. Rose prophetically responded, *"You will not have me now, but perhaps you will be more willing when I am dead."*

Seeing the piety in the little missionary who had brought so much light into everyone's life, the parish priest had a chapel built with an adjoining house, near the convent of *St. Mary of the Roses*. There Rose and a small company of young women could follow a life of the religious. But the company of Nuns received an order from the Holy See to close down the convent as it was too close to the other convent.[14]

Rose returned to her parents' home. There she died on March 6th, 1252. She was seventeen years old. They buried her in the Church of Santa Maria in Podio. But six years later, her body was transferred to the Church of the Convent of *Saint Mary of the Roses*, just as she had prophesied! Although this church was burned down in 1357, her body was intact and is preserved miraculously till this day, incorrupt. Each year her body is carried in solemn procession through the streets of Viterbo. Upon her death, Pope Innocent IV, the same Pope who had refused to allow her to have a convent near the other convent in Viterbo, ordered an investigation to commence into the virtues and sanctity of Rose of Viterbo. However it was not to happen in his pontificate; but one hundred years later, in 1457.

As with many Saints of the past, the faithful proclaimed Rose Saint before the official canonization, because of the virtuous life she shared with them when she was alive and because of the miracles, the lord gave them, through her intercession, before and after she died.

Pope John Paul II told the Youth of the world at a Youth Conference in Denver, Colorado, they are the *Church of Today!* Rose began defending her Pope and her Church when she was twelve. What is the Lord asking of you? Why are you reading this book? Pray! The Lord has such an exciting plan for those who say Yes!

---

[14]This is difficult for us to understand, possibly, because we are not living in those times. Cloistered Nuns, as they all were, subsisted solely on begging and the generosity of the villagers. To have two convents, close by in the same village, could be a burden to the townspeople, they reasoned, or worse could cause the two convents to suffer.

Left: *One of the many Miracles in the life of St. Rose of Viterbo Here she heals a sick young woman.*

Below: *St. Rose of Viterbo meets St. Francis and St. Clare in Glory*

Below:
Incorrupt body of St. Rose of Viterbo in Viterbo, Italy

Dominic Savio

the life of a Saint written by a Saint

Now, when we are living in a time when children are killing children, when children cannot pray in school, when children's favorite toys and video games are of violence and horror, witchcraft and satanism, it is time for them to learn about a teen-ager who strove for and achieved Sainthood; it is time for Saint Dominic Savio. In the year 1950, one teen-ager-Maria Goretti,[1] age twelve was canonized and another-Dominic Savio, age fifteen was beatified. Then in 1954 Dominic Savio was canonized. Did the Lord in His wisdom raise up these two young people to Sainthood to combat the hedonistic philosophy that would pervade the world and the Church, beginning in the 60's?

I have a need to ask *why* we in the Church were not told about these strong, holy role models? In a time when we parents were struck dumb and completely helpless, watching our young drop before our eyes, from drug overdoses, why did we not know about these Saints? Why were our children not being taught in Catholic schools and C.C.D. programs about Saints such as these? Why were these Saints withheld from us, Saints we could hold up to our young, as a contrast to the drug-infested *culture of death*[2] that was being fostered through catchy music? Well, we are taking full responsibility for our young, our right and obligation, as we read in Vatican Council II's Document on Christian Education.[3]

---

[1]Read our chapter on St. Maria Goretti
[2]Pope John Paul II
[3]There are eight different references to the rights of parents as primary teachers of their children in this Document

Above: ***Saint Dominic Savio***
Patron of Youth

Below: ***Saint Dominic Savio's***
father was a blacksmith, and the
little saint was always ready to
help in any way.

Left:
The birthplace of
St. Dominic Savio
in Riva, Italy.

Right:
St. Dominic Savio
would kneel at the
steps in front of
his parish Church
and pray.

The title of this book is entitled *Holy Innocence, The Young and the Saintly;* it could very well be entitled Heroes and Heroines because that is what we are about, bringing you Heroes and Heroines for today, to combat the sick role models being forced on us by the secular world. Man has always needed role models to emulate. Because our young have not grown up learning about the Saints, they have sought and found heroes in the mire of this world's decadence. This Saint is to let our young know that they are precious and born to become Saints. We, the Mystical Body of Christ, are reclaiming our young, the future of our Church, our country, our world.

We ask our young to look into the mirror which Jesus holds up to them, to see themselves as Jesus sees them. This story is not for them to be another Dominic Savio, but to become unique Saints of their own. We want them to know that they have an opportunity to touch lives, just as Dominic did. He, like them, had the trials and tribulations, the temptations and battles our young encounter today, as they journey through this life to eternal life.

We often speak of clusters, God putting people together to do His Will, not only for a particular time and place, but for all time and every place. Saints beget Saints. One of the biographies we referred to, to bring you this powerful holy young Saint, was written by none other than Saint John Bosco, a Saint who had a great impact and involvement in the life of young Dominic Savio, as well as other Saints, some unheralded.

I believe that this true story of Dominic Savio is to challenge the youth of today, with these words of St. John Bosco in the preface:

"If a companion of mine, at my own age, living right here, open to the same, if not bigger, dangers, still found time and means to keep himself a true follower of Jesus Christ, why can't I do the same? But bear well in mind that real religion is not made up of only words; we must come to deeds. On reading something you admire, don't be content to say, "How nice! I like

that!" Say, "I want to strive for those achievements which I most admire in others!"[4]

Out of the muck and mire, a rose blooms

Dominic was born of very poor but holy peasant stock, one of ten children. His parents were from Castelnuovo D'Asti, ten miles outside Turin. When things got desperate they were forced to leave, to find work in a small village outside of Chieri called Riva. There on April 2, 1842, a boy child was born to Charles and Brigid Savio, whom they baptized Dominic. When Dominic was two years old, the family moved once again, to a village near their home town of Castelnuovo d'Asti, Murialdo.

Right from his earliest years, Dominic showed clear signs of piety. His parents said he never gave them cause for the slightest worry, was always obedient and thoughtful of their feelings. At barely four years of age, he swiftly learned his prayers, and could be observed reciting them alone, morning, noon and night. Deeply attached to his mother, he only left her side to go to a small hideaway where he could continue praying unnoticed.

He never began eating without saying Grace. One day, his family unwittingly began eating without first having prayed. Little Dominic cried out, *"Daddy, we haven't asked God to bless our meal yet."*[5] He then proceeded to make the Sign of the Cross and began the prayer the family always recited before eating. All joined in, and after they finished eating, they said the Angelus (as was their custom, morning, noon and night). On another occasion, a guest at their dinner table began eating without first saying Grace. Young Dominic rose and left the table, retiring to a corner of the room. When he was later questioned, as to his strange behavior, he said, *"I didn't dare sit at table with someone who eats like an animal."*

In his biography of this little Saint, Don Bosco speaks not

---

[4]p.24, St. Dominic Savio by St. John Bosco
[5]p.28, St. Dominic Savio by St. John Bosco

only of the extraordinary Grace bestowed upon Dominic, but attributed much of his virtuous life to his parents and their tireless commitment to bring him the treasures of the Church. Their example, their daily, ongoing living out of the Faith, their praying the Rosary and the Angelus as a family, their devout attendance at Mass, their fidelity to the Sacraments, their faithful teaching of the Catechism, bringing Dominic the stark reality of sin with its ultimate destruction of the soul, and the luminous rays of piety with its eternal reward in Heaven, molded him into the Saint he would become.

Father John Zucca said of his pupil, Dominic, that the first time he saw him was when the lad was five years old. As was his custom, Dominic was kneeling on the ground in front of the Church door, waiting for it to open. This was not an isolated case. He could be seen, every morning, praying, his eyes and heart zeroed in on something, or was it Someone, beyond the heavy doors. It was of no consequence, if the ground was muddy and wet from the pouring rain, Dominic knelt and prayed until the church opened.

He was an outstanding student scholastically, as well as spiritually. But as with today, there were rough necks who had not the same focus as Dominic. These young boys attended the same school as Dominic, bent on making trouble their primary occupation. Although out of necessity he had to associate with them in school, he never allowed himself to be coerced into joining them. He resisted them, gently declining to join them in seemingly harmless pranks, which soon turned into willful chaos and ultimate disruption of the classroom. Their mischief unchecked, they turned to harassment of old people on the streets, senseless, malicious destruction of property, and finally stealing. His refusal to join the pack caused him much pain; they taunted him, calling him all sorts of derogatory names. He just walked away, rather than engage in a verbal skirmish which could turn into a physical brawl.

So often we see little boys who live to serve as Altar

Servers, lose their awe and wonder of serving the Mass when they grow older. It was not so with Dominic, who from five years of age reverently served. His life was to attend Daily Mass, so when he was not Altar server, he still devoutly participated in the Mass, adoring his Lord Who was coming to life on the Altar of Sacrifice.

Dominic partakes of the Bread of Angels

He loved all the Sacraments, knowing about them from an early age, and desired to participate in receiving all of them, his eyes and heart set on the priesthood. When he was barely seven, he knew his Catechism by heart and fully understood the teachings of the Church, with spiritual wisdom way beyond his age, especially the Sacraments of Reconciliation and the Eucharist. But in those days, particularly in small country parishes, the age for receiving First Communion was eleven or twelve. Dominic had everything against him, but God. He was small for his age, and the priest hesitated to receive him. The priest consulted other priests. Then considering how well prepared Dominic was and the ardent yearning he had to partake of the Eucharist, he allowed him to receive for the first time the *"Bread of Angels"*[6] and his first *"sweet kiss from Jesus."*[7]

Dominic ran home to tell his mother. He begged pardon from her for anything he may have done to upset her and promised to try to live a more holy life. His mother, deeply moved by this child of hers who had visited upon her nothing by loving concern and affection, tried to hold back the tears as she assured him all was forgiven and asked him to pray that he would always be close to his Lord Whom he would be receiving.

What makes a Saint? Dominic, like other Saints before and after him, had a passion for the Bread of Life, the Eucharist, His Lord truly present, Body, Blood, Soul and Divinity. The day of his First Holy Communion, he rose early. Barely able to wait

---

[6] *"Mortals ate the bread of Angels"* (Psalm 78:25)
[7] St. Therese of Lisieux, the Little Flower

for that glorious moment when he and the Lord would become one, he went to the church and knelt on the ground, outside waiting for the doors to open. The Mass, including his first Penance, lasted five hours. Dominic never forgot that day, and when he spoke of it, years later, his eyes misted as he said, *"For me it was the best day - it was a great day."*[8]

St. John Bosco advised those about to receive First Holy Communion to take St. Dominic Savio as their Patron Saint, following the resolutions he made that day and ensued all the days of his life:

(1) I will go to penance often and receive Communion as often as my confessor allows;

(2) I will keep Feast Days holy;

(3) My friends shall be Jesus and Mary;

(4) Death but not sin.

Cardinal Salotti, defender of St. Dominic Savio's cause said: *"These resolutions are evidently the most remarkable legacy left by Dominic to the youth of today."*[9]

Dominic - from trials and temptations to Sainthood

He was determined to get an education so that he would be able to serve God someday as a priest, even if he had to walk ten miles a day to do so. So each morning before there were lights burning in any of the homes he passed, ten year old Dominic trudged to elementary school. No matter, the rain pouring, the wind tossing his frail frame about, Dominic was prepared to brave any opposing force to get closer to his Lord and eternity with Him, and he knew that was through education, for you cannot love someone you do not know.

When a man questioned him one day, was he not afraid to walk alone, he answered, he was not alone, his Guardian Angel was walking beside him. When he was asked was he not tired, making that trip, each day, his response always was, referring to

---

[8]p.34, St. Dominic Savio by St. John Bosco
[9]p.34, St. Dominic Savio by St. John Bosco

God, the Creator, *"My Master pays me well. He repays even a glass of water given in His Name."*

Now, you would think a boy of such great spirituality would not be vulnerable, open to temptation, wouldn't you? I think the Lord allows our Saints to have trials, and sometimes fall or almost fall, so that the Saints are touchable and therefore easier to follow. The walk to school was filled with dangers, worse than those of the body. Our Lord said,

"Do not be afraid of those who kill the body but cannot kill the soul; fear him rather who can destroy both body and soul in hell."[10]

In the heat of summer, some of Dominic's classmates liked to go swimming in the nude. Not only were there physical dangers open to them, but more serious spiritual ones. They persisted in their coaxing of Dominic to go with them. He resisted their supplications, tears streaming down his face, imploring them to not to go swimming. But one day he succumbed and was about to join them. When he quickly realized the imminent danger to their souls, as well as the possible threats to their bodies, he tried to dissuade them. He later grieved for the possible risk to his own immortal soul that he had foolishly exposed himself to, by momentarily giving in to these supposed friends. When they again brazenly taunted him, calling him all sorts of names, in an attempt to trick him into doing their will, he explained that what they were doing could lead to sin and he was not about to offend God out of friendship to them.

Although he was uncompromising in his dedication to God and his Church, he was a gentle evangelist, speaking lovingly, not harshly. With this sweet disposition and sincere heart, he made such an impression on his classmates they would stop using offensive language when they saw him approaching. Whereas he was loving to everyone, he never allowed himself to be tempted

---

[10]Mt. 10:28

again, avoiding every incident of sin by giving a wide berth to those who chose to be irresponsibly enmeshed in temptation and finally sin.

In 1852, the family moved once again to another town outside Turin, called Mondonio. In his new school, Dominic would encounter new friends, new challenges, and new tests! There was an incident where one of the students was guilty of an infraction which would result in his expulsion. Knowing of the consequences, the guilty party and his friends decided to accuse Dominic of the crime. They were able to convince the priest. Believing Dominic was the culprit, he came storming into the room. He had Dominic kneel in the center of the classroom while he berated him: *"Don't you know, I could have you expelled for doing such a thing? You're lucky it's your first time. Make sure, its your last."*

Although Dominic could have cleared his name, he offered no defense. When the next day, the guilty parties were exposed, the priest questioned Dominic why he chose to remain silent and take the punishment due the others. To which, Dominic replied he was aware the other boy would have been expelled, and he felt because it was his first offense the priest would go easy on him. Besides, he insisted, Jesus had been falsely accused and said nothing right up to death on the Cross. When Cardinal Salotti later spoke of this incident, he said he saw it as *"a humiliation freely accepted before teacher and classmates, an act of charity towards the real culprits, and an act of love for God which makes him imitate Christ silent before His accusers."*

Dominic and St. John Bosco meet

Dominic received the Sacrament of Confirmation in 1853, at the age of eleven. God was formulating His plan of holiness for Dominic Savio. The Lord had placed him in the hands of holy parents who had nurtured his faith in God. Now, it was time for another Saint to enter Dominic's life. We have said over and over again that there are Saints and Saint-makers. Dominic had been received as a full member of the Church through the

Above: *St. Dominic receives his first Holy Communion*

Above: *St. Dominic Savio loved St. John Bosco*

Left: *The oratory of St. John Bosco in Turin, where St. John Bosco brought him.*

Right: *St. Dominic Savio forms the Company of the Immaculate Conception at the Oratory of St. John Bosco in Turin, Italy.*

Sacrament of Confirmation. He was ready for the next step.

If you remember, Dominic's parents were originally from Castelnuovo. It just happened (holy coincidence?) that Don Bosco was originally from Castelnuovo. Don Bosco was already well-known for his Oratory and his work with the young. Dominic, as well as all the citizens of the area, looked upon Don Bosco as the *local boy who made good*. Dominic would tell all his friends his greatest aspiration was to meet Don Bosco and be admitted into his Oratory. When he was asked why, he simply replied he wanted to become a priest, *"what better way to save his soul and do good for others."*

It was 1854, Dominic was twelve and it was time; so the Lord used Dominic's parish priest to speak of him to Don Bosco, who just happened to be in guess where - Castelnuovo! The priest related Dominic's great piety and eagerness to learn, whereupon Don Bosco agreed to meet him. Upon hearing this good news, Dominic left immediately for Castelnuovo with his father. Boy and teacher met, and when Don Bosco asked him why he wanted to go to Turin with him, Dominic answered, *"With God's Grace, I very much want to become a priest!"*

St. Bosco handed Dominic a copy of *Catholic Readings* and assigned him a page to read. He said if he could recite it tomorrow, he would bring him to Turin. Dominic went off, while Don Bosco and his father spoke. Eight minutes later, he returned and recited the page by heart. He had not only memorized the page, it was obvious he had a keen understanding of its message. Needless to say, Don Bosco took Dominic with him the next day, and a love and friendship began between the priest of thirty-eight and the boy of twelve.

October, 1854, Dominic became a student at the Oratory of St. Francis de Sales in Turin. When Dominic arrived at the Oratory, he went to Don Bosco's room, to pledge his undying obedience to him, as his superior. Don Bosco noticed Dominic deeply interested in a banner on the wall with a cherished saying by St. Francis de Sales. He asked Dominic to translate the Latin saying: *Da Mihi Animas, Caetera Tolle* into Italian. Dominic replied: *"Lord give me souls, take away the rest."*[11] Dominic was pensive for a minute and replied: *"I see! Here you don't do business for money but in souls! I understand. I hope you will deal with my soul."*[12]

[Do you ever wonder what God is doing with you and through you, this your time on earth? I don't think any of the Saints gave that much thought. They only lived to please God, and in so doing God used them. Can we see another Saint here in God's plan? St. Francis de Sales had inspired Don Bosco, and in turn Don Bosco would inspire Dominic.]

Believing that obedience is the path to Sainthood, Dominic listened intently to his superiors, never questioning, just obeying to the fullest of his ability, always wanting to do more. Dominic stayed close to Don Bosco in an effort to learn how to serve God. He wanted to know all the rules, so that he could never hurt God by inadvertently disobeying his superiors. He, like many of the Saints, believed that it was through obedience to his superiors he was doing God's Will.

Cast the first stone at me!

The Oratory was not filled with boys from finishing schools but included many street children who had been beaten, brutalized, abandoned, used and abused. And although change was coming about, sometimes it was quicker with some, and slower with others. One day, Dominic came upon two angrily boys who began by first calling each other foul names. When it turned into slandering each other's family, it looked as if they were about to engage in some serious stone-throwing. Now, anyone will tell you the one who gets hurt is the one who gets in between two having a fight. Dominic did not think of the cost; he knew he had only to end the fight, before someone was gravely hurt. He came between them. Taking a crucifix from around his

---

[11]p.53 St. Dominic Savio by St. John Bosco
[12]p.53 St. Dominic Savio by St. John Bosco

neck, he said, *"Before you fight, look at this, both of you, and say, 'Jesus was innocent, and died forgiving His killers; I am a sinner, and I am going to offend Him by willful revenge.' And then you must throw a stone at me."*

Now, these boys were both bigger and stronger than he. He chose to kneel in front of the angriest boy and said, *"Now throw the first stone. Hit me hard on the head!"* Now, Dominic was loved by almost all the boys at the Oratory. The boy refused, saying, *"I have nothing against you. I will protect you against anyone who would hurt you.* When he repeated his prior order to the other boy, he too professed his love and high regard for Dominic and refused to throw a stone at him.

Then Dominic turned to them shaking with emotion and said, *"You are both ready to face serious danger to save me, only a simple creature, but you haven't the strength to forgive a silly insult made in school to save your own souls, which cost your Savior His Blood, and you are going to shed that blood."*

Not only did they forgive one another, because of Dominic's love and bravery they asked for a priest where they could confess their sins against each other. Dominic never spoke of this, and had not the two boys spoken of it no one would know, till today.

His way to school was paved with temptations, one after the other, most of which he battled successfully, resisting their high-pressure pleading to stay away from school, just once! One day, when the teasing became more than he could withstand, he was about to give in and be truant from school. But suddenly (was it his Guardian Angel?) he realized he was falling into serious temptation and refused, saying *"If you were really my friends you would not want me to displease God and my superiors. I'm sorry I gave in, and if you tease me again, you'll never be my friends."* Not only did they return to school with him, they never tried to coerce him into praying truant from school again.

At the end of the year, although Dominic was to rank top

in his class and was promoted to the next grade level, his health was so weakened, he had to take private lessons at the Oratory. And his cross, never complaining, there were those who were envious and called him names, accusing him of being Don Bosco's pet student.

"I want to become a Saint"

Six months had passed since he had entered the Oratory and Dominic heard Don Bosco preach on the road to Sainthood. There were three points that Don Bosco made that were deeply imprinted on Dominic's heart:

(1) It is God's Will that we all become Saints

(2) It is not hard to become a Saint

(3) There is a great reward in Heaven for those who become Saints.

Dominic was so moved by Don Bosco's sermon, he became pensive and unusually quiet. Fearing he was getting sick, again Don Bosco inquired about his health. Dominic said it was that he never knew it was so easy to become a Saint and now that he knows he wanted to work at it day and night. Like the great Saints before him, Don Bosco cautioned Dominic he was to be a cheerful Saint, steadfastly doing his daily tasks and spiritual exercises with joy. But Dominic never relented in his quest for Sainthood. One day, Don Bosco told him he wanted to give him a gift, to which Dominic responded *"The only gift I want is that you make me a Saint! I want to give myself entirely to the Lord, forever to the Lord! If I don't I shall be a failure! God wants me to become a Saint and I must become one!"* On another Feast Day, when Don Bosco again offered Dominic a gift, his answer was unflinchingly the same, *"Please save my soul and make me a Saint."*

As Don Bosco sensed the soul of a future Saint in Dominic, he began to give him spiritual exercises to do. He told him to strive to win souls for God, because those souls were ransomed by the Blood of the Lamb on the Cross.

How do you feel when someone uses the Name of the

Lord in vain, blaspheming against the Holy Spirit? When Dominic would hear people offending God in this vile manner, he would bow his head sadly and repeat over and over again, *"Praised be Jesus Christ!"* One day, one of his friends overheard him saying something, but he couldn't make out what he was saying. When he asked Dominic, he replied, *"Didn't you hear that workman use the Name of the Lord in vain? I was tempted to go up to him and say something, but it would only have made things worse, so instead I donned my hat and said, 'Praised be Jesus Christ!' In this way, I pray I can make up for the hurts suffered by my Lord when His Name is taken in vain."* One time, he couldn't resist going up to an elderly man who had taken our Lord's name in vain. When he lovingly and gently told him how he wounded Jesus when he blasphemed, the old man said he was sorry, and that he would try real hard to refrain what had become a bad habit.

Dominic often spoke of going to far-off places to save souls. He was most concerned with the souls in England, who as he said, were waiting for someone to save their souls. He would often say if he had the strength he would go there and shed, if necessary, every ounce of his blood, to lead them to God by preaching and good example.

He was deeply concerned because parents did not take the time to teach their children about the treasures of our Faith which lead to holiness, did not tell their families stories about the lives of the Saints. He would gather young people and tell them stories about these Heroes of our Church. He often said that when he became a seminarian he would gather all the children and teach them the Catholic Faith. He cried that so many of God's children were lost for all time because they had no one to teach them the truths of the Faith. He like his mentor, Don Bosco, who like his mentor St. Francis de Sales, believed that the greatest enemy and threat to the Church is ignorance.

[I wonder how many children who commit senseless crimes would do so, if they knew how much Jesus loved them

Right: *St. Dominic Savio dreamed about the Pope, Pius IX.*
In the dream, St. Dominic saw the Pope carrying a torch for England, and he saw a great triumph for the Catholic Church there.

Left:
St. Dominic Savio receives his Viaticum.
He died March 9, 1857.

Right:
St. Dominic Savio in Glory

and died just for them? Are we failing in our duties toward the future leaders of our Church, our country, our world? What role models are we giving them? How can you teach them to love a God they do not know, to obey and adore a God they do not know?]

He would always reward his students in his Catechism class with some small reward or gift for a lesson well learned or for attending Mass, or going to confession, or for good attendance at Catechism class. It worked! Making the Sign of the Cross reverently was important to him, he would ask the children to do it slowly, standing in front of them so that they could imitate him. To Dominic and most of the Saints, making the Sign of the Cross was to summon and honor the Trinity - God the Father, Jesus His Son and the Holy Spirit!

Lead me not into an incident of sin

As I read about Dominic and those days, I can see the clear parallels with today. One day, Dominic saw a crowd of young people gathering about this man. As he drew nearer, he could hear the man telling some very crude jokes. Many left, but others stayed, enthralled by the charming, witty manner in which he spun his yarns so mixed with humor, the less sensitive could not see how deeply he was pulling them down into hell. Now, you have to picture this young teen-ager, Dominic, slight and gentle of spirit, bravely and boldly standing up to this eloquent speaker who now had the crowd mesmerized. Dominic turned to the crowd and demanded they leave this man, as he was about the business of destroying souls. When they protested, he made them laugh, he replied, "Yes right to hell."

[Do we keep comedy television programs on because they are funny, relaxing, even when they become lewd and blasphemous? Are we laughing ourselves and our children straight to hell? Oh, I know this is a *politically incorrect* statement to make today; but unless we have young Dominics and older Don Boscos, many souls will perish; and they will perish in hell, no matter what some dissident theologians say, for hell is real and it is final.]

"Mary, I want to always be your son."

Friends at the Oratory spoke of Dominic's deep love for the Blessed Mother; they would spy him praying before her statue, before and after Mass, sometimes for hours, motionless. It was 1854, and the Feast of the Immaculate Conception was fast approaching. Don Bosco asked the boys to prepare for their Heavenly Mother's Feast Day with the love and care of true sons, asking her intercession for petitions they were in most *need* of, and her motherly protection in their endeavor to live holy lives.

The world and the Church was holding its breath. Pantheism had been adorning the unsuspecting with the cloak of pride with its heresy that God is created in the image of man and therefore can be like God. This torrent of delusion had all but swallowed up the Church, drowning her unknowing children in the mire of deceit and error. It was time for Pope Pius IX to declare the Dogma of the Immaculate Conception.

[We have those within the Church (with their new theology of New Age) and without the Church (like the Mormons who falsely advertise their belief in Jesus, but instead profess *"As man is, God once was. As God is, man may become."* Is it time for another strong definition of that which we believe that there is only one God in Three Persons, Father, Son and Holy Spirit, and there is no other God in Heaven or on earth, and that only Jesus and the Blessed Mother were born without the stain of original sin?]

Dominic wanted to do something really special for His Heavenly Mother Mary. He said he needed to do it right away, or there wouldn't be enough time. It was nine months before his death. He began a novena. He wrote nine resolutions and acts of piety on individual pieces of paper, one for each day, as a gift to the Blessed Mother. He made a general confession of all his sins, and then received Holy Communion. That evening, after evening prayers, under the advisement of Don Bosco, Dominic spent time kneeling before the statue of the Blessed Mother. He prayed, over and over again, *"Mary, I give you my heart. Always keep it yours. Jesus, Mary, always be my friends. I beg you, let me die rather than to be so unfortunate as to commit a single sin.*"[13]

In addition to the great impact that his living out a life of holiness, had on the other students of the Oratory, one of the things Dominic is most remembered for is the group he organized called the *Company of the Immaculate Conception.* Their focus was to gain the help of the great Mother of God in life and at the hour of death. This group was not only one of prayer and devotions, they assisted Don Bosco doing all the menial tasks necessary around the Oratory, not only sweeping floors but also reaching out to those young boys in most need of help, those the world had discarded, the unwanted. Perhaps this is the most meaningful work done at the Oratory, giving these unloved and uncared for children, belief in God through the love generated by Don Bosco, Dominic Savio and many others who passed through the portals of St. Francis de Sales Oratory in Turin. You can just hear their little hearts murmuring, *"There is a God, and I know He loves me!"*

When in 1859, Don Bosco began the now world-wide Salesian Congregation, all the original members of the Company of the Immaculate Conception were there, except Dominic Savio who was already with Jesus and Mary Whom he so dearly loved. But as love never dies, I can just see Dominic, pointing out all his friends to Jesus and Mary, pleading their cause and those of the boys who would follow.

Dominic had had a holy earthly mother whom he dearly loved, but he gave his heart to his Heavenly Mother. Whenever he had free time, he either read his books or prayed in church, especially for the Poor Souls in Purgatory. All this he did in the name of Mary, his Mother. He kept the mirror of his soul, his eyes, pure for Mother Mary. Whenever he and his friends were

---

[13]p.55 St. Dominic Savio by St. John Bosco

walking to church, and they spotted some attractive young girls, the boys would stare at them. Then seeing Dominic's eyes downcast, averting the girls, they would become angry, teasing, "What do you have eyes for if not for looking?" To which he would reply, *"I will use them to see the face of Our Blessed Mother, if by the Grace of God I am worthy of Heaven."*

Dominic strives for holiness for himself and others

If you think it was an easy thing being different, resisting the temptations that are ever-present for a young man seeking holiness, have another guess. There were times, he had to try so hard to avert situations and objects that could have endangered his immortal soul, he would get terrible headaches. But his friends all testified that he never succumbed to the temptation to look upon anything that would offend God. Saints are molded by God through the Saint's cooperation with God's Grace. Knowing the danger into which the eyes can lead you, Dominic said, *"The eyes are two windows through which we can let anything enter. We can let an Angel or a devil pass to take control of our hearts."*[14]

One day, he came upon his friends intently looking at a magazine. When he peered over their shoulders to see what was so fascinating, he saw the most disgusting, irreligious cartoons that would have made a pagan blush. He severely chastised them saying, *"Our Lord says we can soil our souls with a single evil glance, and you gloat over these dirty things."*

In a time when *children* are being shown pornographic material in the name of Sex Education, and handed contraceptives so that they can practice *safe sex*, where the word *Chastity* has been all but wiped from the face of the earth, along with God the Father, allegiance to the flag of the United States, prayer in schools, any mention of God because it offends atheists, a time when the sinful is no longer sin, and righteousness is a joke, we need to ask St. Dominic and St. Don

---

[14]p.93 St. Dominic Savio by St. John Bosco

Bosco to pray for us and the generations to follow. Dominic prayed, *"Mary, I always want to be your son. Let me die before I commit a single sin against Chastity."* We must fight the enemy of God who is ensnaring our young and not so young into his tentacles of sin and damnation. If Don Bosco and Dominic could do it in a big, sin-filled city like Turin where it wasn't safe to walk the streets, day or night, in a time when people were so destitute they couldn't feed their families, often sending them out into the streets to fend for themselves, then we can do it; we must do it; we will do it!

Dominic's strength -
The Sacraments of Penance and the Holy Eucharist
Dominic heard Don Bosco say, "Boys, if you want to stay on the path to Heaven, do three things:
(1) go to confession regularly;
(2) receive Communion often;
(3) choose a regular confessor to whom you can unburden your heart. Don't change him, unless you have to."

Whereas before he came to the Oratory, he was going to confession and receiving Communion once a month, after hearing this sermon, he went to confession and received Communion every two weeks, then every week; then his confessor seeing the leaps he was making in his spiritual life, he directed him to receive Holy Communion three times a week and then every day.

Dominic had ultimate trust in his confessor, saying, *"The confessor is the doctor of the soul. People change their doctor when they no longer have confidence in him, or realize they are beyond being cured. I trust my confessor fully. With fatherly concern and kindness he cares for my soul. I have no hurt he cannot heal."* Dominic said that when he was worried, he went to his confessor, and through him, God spoke to him.

Dominic loved to spend an hour before the Blessed Sacrament saying, *"What else do I need to be happy? Nothing in this world but to be able to see Him Whom I now see by faith and adore on the altar.*"[15]   He would make at least one visit a day, bringing other boys with him. To make these times before his Lord, more meaningful, he would say the Little Crown of the Sacred Heart - a prayer that is recited in reparation for the insults hurled against Christ by heretics, infidels, and unworthy Christians, and he drew up a list of intentions:

Sunday	in honor of the Blessed Trinity;
Monday	for those who help me materially and spiritually;
Tuesday	in honor of St. Dominic and my Guardian Angel;
Wednesday	to Our Lady of Sorrows for the conversion of sinners
Thursday	for the Poor Souls in Purgatory
Friday	in honor of Jesus' Passion
Saturday	in honor of Mary most holy, to obtain her protection in life and at death.

Although he was a happy young man, nothing gave him the joy that the Eucharist gave him. Whenever he saw a priest pass by, carrying the Eucharist to the dying, he would immediately go down on his knees and time permitting, accompany the priest. One particular day, there had been a down-pour of rain, and the streets were all muddy.   When Dominic spotted the priest carrying the Eucharist to the sick, he went down on his knees. His friend ridiculed him, insisting Jesus did not want Dominic to soil his clothes. Dominic replied, *"My knees and clothes belong to God and should do Him service. When I am near Him I would gladly crawl in the mud to pay Him homage. I'd jump into a furnace if I could get a spark of that infinite love which made Him give us this great Sacrament."*

Another time, he perceived a soldier standing at attention when the Blessed Sacrament was being processed past him. Not wanting to be rude or forward, Dominic placed his handkerchief on the ground and motioned to the soldier to use it to kneel upon. The soldier got so flustered, he knelt on the dirty cobblestones.

---

[15]p.84 St. Dominic Savio by St. John Bosco

There were times when Dominic either received Holy Communion or was in adoration of the Blessed Sacrament, that he appeared so suspended in time, as if in a state of ecstasy, he would have remained in the church indefinitely, had not the custodian awakened him. One day, Dominic had missed breakfast, class and lunch. When Don Bosco inquired, no one had seen him; he was in the study hall or dormitory. Don Bosco went to look for him in church. He found Dominic on the altar, "immovable as a rock...one foot was resting on the other; one hand was placed on a lectern, the other against his chest. His face was rigidly fixed on the tabernacle. His lips were not moving." Don Bosco called to him. There was no response. When he shook him, then Dominic asked, *"Oh, is Mass over already?"* Don Bosco showed him the time; it was two o'clock in the afternoon. Dominic begged his forgiveness. Don Bosco told him to tell no one what had happened.

Don Bosco tells of another time when after Mass, as he was giving thanks to the Lord, he heard what appeared to be arguing. He went to investigate. There was Dominic speaking and then pausing, as if he were listening to someone. Don Bosco did not hear all that was said, but he recalled Dominic saying clearly, *"Yes my God, I have told you already and I will tell you again, I love you and I will love you till death. If you see that I am going to offend you, let me die first! Yes, death but not sin."*[16]

When Don Bosco asked Dominic what he saw when he was lost in time, he replied that he sees such beauty, unlike anything he has ever beheld, that he becomes lost in time. One day, Dominic excitedly begged Don Bosco to follow him. Knowing that his urgency was not something to be ignored, from past experiences, Don Bosco followed close by as Dominic dashed down one street, then another, through alleys till they arrived at this one house. A woman rushed over to Don Bosco

---

[16]p.116 St. Dominic Savio by St. John Bosco

and begged him to hear her husband's confession. He was dying. She said that he had been Catholic and had left the Faith to become a Protestant but now wanted to die Catholic. The dying man unburdened his soul; he barely received the Sacrament of Extreme Unction (the Anointing of the Sick) when he died. When Don Bosco asked Dominic how he knew about this man, Dominic looked so distressed, tears welling up in his eyes, that he did not pursue it any further.

It became more and more difficult to keep his ecstasies from the other boys. One day, in the courtyard, when someone started to speak of the reward in Heaven, awaiting those who have not lost their innocence, it was enough to raise Dominic's soul immediately to God[17] and he went into ecstasy, collapsing stiffly into his comrades arms.   The ecstasies came indiscriminately in the study hall, in the classroom, to and from school.

He kept telling Don Bosco he wished he could speak to the Pope, before dying.   When Don Bosco asked him what he wanted to tell the Pope, he replied, *"If I could speak to the Pope, I would tell him that in the midst of all his troubles he must not stop taking special care of England. God is preparing a great triumph for the Catholic Church there."*   When Don Bosco pressed him to tell him how he knew of this, Dominic begged Don Bosco to tell no one, so that they would not make fun of him. He said, he had a vision (he called it a distraction), one morning after Communion, when he was making his thanksgiving. He saw an enormous plain with people covered by a thick blanket of fog, confused, floundering, lost. When he inquired who they were, he was told this was England. Then Dominic saw Pope Pius IX, as he had seen him in pictures. He walked toward the people carrying a flaming torch. As he approached an area, the fog lifted, and in its place was a clear bright day filled with rays of sun, streaming down from Heaven.

---

[17]p.118 St. Dominic Savio by St. John Bosco

Then Dominic heard, *"This is the Catholic religion which must enlighten the English."*[18] When Don Bosco recounted this to Pope Pius IX, in 1858, he said that it just confirmed his desire to continue striving vigorously for England.

There are many occurences in Dominic's life that Don Bosco recorded, but left for others to write about. One such incident was reported by his family, after Dominic died. One day, Dominic begged to be allowed to go home. He said his mother was very ill and Our Lady wanted her to be cured. Don Bosco asked, how he knew. But seeing his reluctance, Don Bosco agreed, without pressing him for an explanation. Dominic left for Mondonio. On his way, he met up with his father who was on his way to fetch a doctor. He expressed surprise at seeing Dominic. But the boy just told him to go to *grandma's* house, and hurried on to his mother's side. When he got there, the mid-wives, having labored long and hard, had given up; she was dying and the baby with her. Dominic ran into the room, jumped on the bed and embraced his mother, placing a green scapular around her neck, telling her, *"I'm going now. You'll be all right."* His mother told everyone that the Blessed Mother, through the green scapular, saved her life and the life of the baby. When he arrived back at the Oratory, he told Don Bosco that his mother was saved. Our Lady cured her. When his mother wanted to return the scapular to Dominic, he insisted she keep it, and share it with other women who are faced with the same threat to their lives that she had known. He said that as Our Lady had saved her life through the scapular, so she would save and cure others.

Dominic's life - an ongoing preparation for a holy death.

At the Oratory the boys would make a monthly "Exercise for a Happy Death." It was a devotion blessed by Pope Pius IX with many indulgences. It consisted of preparing carefully for confession and receiving Holy Communion, as if it was for the

---

[18]p.118 St. Dominic Savio by St. John Bosco

last time. Each time they made the Exercise, Dominic would half jokingly declare, *"Do not say, `For the one among us.'* Say *"For Dominic Savio, who will be the first among us to die."* He would repeat this often.

Toward the end of April, 1856, he asked Don Bosco what he should do, and how he could spend May being holy. Don Bosco told him to do his work cheerfully, teach his friends about Mother Mary, and behave in such a way that he could receive Communion every day, worthily. When Dominic agreed, he then asked what favor he should request of Blessed Mother. To which Don Bosco replied he should ask her to help him become a Saint, ask her to assist him at the last moments of his life that he might die a holy death, and bring him to Heaven to dwell with her and her Son. Dominic dedicated every hour of his day, every work, every prayer, every penance to Blessed Mother, and when he was asked by one of the other students, what he would do next year, he replied he would wait till next year, if he was still alive. So, we can see the little future Saint knew he was dying and he was preparing for that great and glorious day when the Blessed Mother would come to take him home.

Don Bosco, too, was aware Dominic was dying; he could see his health declining at an accelerated pace, his strength rapidly ebbing away. He consulted the doctors who said that his body was frail, his mind was alert and sharp, it was his spiritual life that was killing him. When Don Bosco inquired what he could do, the doctor said the best thing was to allow him to go to Heaven, as he was so ready; but should he want him to live longer, relieve him of his studies and give him little physical tasks that were undemanding. His hope was that this possibly would take Dominic's mind off the spiritual which caused him to go into ecstasy, draining and debilitating him physically to the point of killing him. It is said that Dominic would be in a state of ecstasy as long as *six hours* at a time.

[Although the gift of ecstasy is being in the presence of the Divine or Blessed Mother, there was always a price to pay, a physical price. As it was with Dominic, it was likewise with other mystics we have written about, like St. Clare of Montefalco, whom the doctors told the Nuns to have Clare walk so that she would not go into ecstasy, as it was draining her of life. Of course, it was to no avail.]

Dominic's fatal illness was puzzling to doctors as well as Don Bosco. He was small in stature, (Don Bosco's pet name for him was little Dominic), but he wasn't unhealthy. There was no sign of a threatening illness, no history of Tuberculosis in his family (which was the prime killer of his day); his father lived to be seventy-five years old. He, like his mentor Don Bosco had no more to give. When Don Bosco was dying, they asked the doctors what was wrong with him. He replied it was no great illness or disease. He was just out of steam. He was like an oil lamp without oil.[19] Like Don Bosco, Dominic had done all there was for him to do on earth and there was nothing left; he had no more strength.

Dominic Savio had been a bright candle, like the candle that enters our dark churches on the vigil of Easter, bringing hope and joy into our dark lives. It would appear that God snuffed out this candle while it was still burning, as we do when the Vigil Easter Mass begins. But, as with this Easter Candle, the effects of the candle that entered the Church through *"little Dominic"* has continued to bring light into a world hell-bent on darkness. Dominic Savio is the sign of what we can be! I would like to address the youth of our Church! Pope John Paul II said that you, the youth, are the Church! What kind of a Church do we have? What kind of a Church will we have? Is God asking you to be a Dominic Savio of today? Do you have the courage this young boy had? Do you believe in life after death? Do we believe that we have *Life Eternal* through Jesus Christ? Then set your eyes on that which is *Above*. All the wealth of this world, the material goods, the fame, the power is passing away, only

---

[19]chapter on Don Bosco, *Saints and other Powerful Men in the Church*, by Bob and Penny Lord

Jesus and His promise will never leave us alone and destitute. What do you say? Pray to St. Dominic Savio.

Don Bosco had no recourse but to obey the doctors' orders; he sent him home. This was one of the hardest things he had to do, as Dominic was such a joy to him. He and the doctors hoped this would be a place where, away from his studies and all the activities of the Oratory, he would be able to regain his strength. A few days after having left with his father, he returned to the Oratory. Dominic's illness did not require him to stay in bed, all the time. He attended class when he could; he helped out in the infirmary, saying this was his greatest joy, caring for his sick brothers.

Dominic developed a persistent cough which further weakened him. Now, the doctors insisted he be sent home, and Don Bosco obeyed. When he told Dominic, he inquired why Don Bosco was sending him away. When Don Bosco questioned him, did he not want to go home and be with his parents, he answered, *"I want to end my life at the Oratory."*[20] When Don Bosco tried to reassure him (and himself) that he would return when he was well, Dominic said, *"No, no, Father, I will go, but I will never return."*

Dominic had always been Don Bosco's shadow, but this last night he never left his side, asking questions,

"What is the best thing a boy can do to gain merit with God?

Don Bosco replied, *"Offer God your sufferings."*

"Can I be sure my sins are forgiven?" Dominic persisted.

"I can assure you in God's Name they are."

"Can I be sure of my salvation?"

"Yes, you can, with God's Grace, which will not be lacking."

"If the devil were to tempt me, what should I answer?"

"Tell him that you have already sold your soul to Jesus,

---

[20]p.128 St. Dominic Savio by St. John Bosco

*and He has bought it with His Blood. If he keeps on bothering
you, ask him what he has done for your soul. Jesus had died to
free you from sin and take you with Him to Heaven."*

*"Can I see my parents and my schoolmates from
Heaven?"*

*"Yes you will see the Oratory and your parents, and you
will know everything that concerns them, and so many other
wonderful things besides."*

"Can I visit sometimes?"

"If those visits are for God's glory, yes."[21]

Dominic kept asking questions until he finally dropped off
to sleep. He wasn't afraid of dying. I believe that he, like the
Savior he adored, was sad at leaving his loved ones but excitedly
wanting to know about his new Home. He had prepared all his
short fifteen years for this journey and he wanted to be prepared,
just as someone going to a far-off place, getting last minute
instructions.

Dominic says good-by to his Oratory family.

Morning came and Dominic began to prepare for his
departure. First, he made the *"Exercise for a Happy Death."*[22]
He explained that he wanted to do it, well, to prepare him for a
happy death, and so that if he were to die on the way home, he
would have already received Communion.

Others said that they had the deep awareness, watching
him at prayer in church, that he would one day become a Saint.
He carefully packed his belongings, as if this was the last time he
would see them. He said good-by to each of his friends, begging
forgiveness for anything he had done or failed to do. He told
them to work on the salvation of their souls; he affirmed them,
but challenged them to be more. He gave them spiritual advice,
his eyes gleaming with the knowledge of where he was going.
He told his companions of the Company of Mary to be faithful to

---

[21]p.128 St. Dominic Savio by St. John Bosco
[22]p.176 of this book - see reference to this Exercise

their Mother and she would bring them through any crisis in their lives. He insisted on paying back even the smallest debt, saying he wanted all his debts cleared up so that he would not have to include them in his accounting before the Lord.

At last, it was time to say good-by to Don Bosco. *"Since you don't want this poor carcass of mine, I'll have to take it back to Mondonio. But it would only have burdened you for a few days, and all would soon be over. God's Will be done! If you go to Rome, remember what I told you to tell the Pope about England. Pray for me that I may have a good death. We will see each other in Heaven."*

As he was about to depart, he waved to all his friends, telling them he would see them in Heaven. Then he asked Don Bosco for a present he could remember him by. When Don Bosco asked him what he wished, he replied,

"You told me once that the Pope gave you plenary indulgences for the hour of death. Put my name among those who can gain that indulgence."

Then Dominic walked away from the Oratory. This was the home he had known for three of his fifteen years. He left, never to return.

The days ahead, at home were filled with pain, patiently accepted by the little soldier of Christ. Finally, he turned to his father and said, *"Let's call in the Divine Physician now. I want to go to confession and receive Communion."* After he received the Viaticum, he could be heard saying, *"Jesus, Mary, yes, you will always be my friends. I say again and again, death but not sin!"*

After he made his thanksgiving, he said, *"Now I am happy. I have to make the long trip to eternity, but, with Jesus to keep me company, I am not afraid. Oh, tell everyone, tell it often, if Jesus is your Companion and Friend, there is nothing to fear, not even death."*

After four days of blood-letting and etc., Dominic seemed to rally. The doctor joyfully assured everyone the crisis had passed and Dominic would soon fully recover. Unimpressed with the doctor's enthusiasm, Dominic smiled and said, *"The world is beaten. All I need is a careful appearance before God."*

He gently turned to his parents and asked for the Anointing of the Sick. Although they did not agree with him, they called in the priest. Just as he was to receive the *Last Rites*,[23] Dominic prayed, *"My God, forgive me my sins. I love You, and I want to love You forever. May this Sacrament, which in Your infinite mercy You are letting me receive, cancel all the sins I have committed by sight and hearing, by my mouth, hands and feet. May my body and soul be sanctified by the merits of Your Holy Passion. Amen."*

The priest gave him the Papal Blessing. Dominic recited the act of contrition to himself, answered the prayers of the priest, and received the Holy Father's blessing and a Plenary Indulgence. He kept whispering "Deo Gratias" - *"Thanks be to God."* Holding the Crucifix close, he repeated a verse he loved to say,

"Lord, take my freedom, I give it to thee.
My body and all its strength are Thine
All that I have You gave to me,
To bow to Thy Will be mine."

It is the evening of March 9, 1857, no one believed Dominic was dying, he looked so happy, so peaceful. The priest and the family were confused; Dominic was commending his soul to God.

Dominic's breathing became labored. He asked the priest for a remembrance. When he asked what he could give him, Dominic replied, something to comfort him. "Remember the Passion of Jesus." Dominic thanked him, and then prayed, *"The Passion of Jesus will always be in my mind, on my lips, and in my heart. Jesus, Mary and Joseph, may I breath forth my soul in peace with You."*

---

[23]another expression for Anointing of the Sick

Dominic fell asleep and after an hour, he looked over to his parents and said, *"Dad, it's time. Take my prayer book and read me the prayers for a happy death."* Overcome by grief, his mother left the room sobbing. Although this was the most painful thing he would ever have to do, his father forced himself to read the prayers. At the end of each Litany of the Dying, Dominic would pray, *"Merciful Jesus, have mercy on me."* When his father came to the words, *"When at length my soul, admitted to Your presence, shall first behold the immortal splendor of Your Majesty, reject it not, but receive me into the Loving Bosom of Your mercy, where I may ever sing Your praises."* Dominic gasped, *"Yes, that's all I want, Dad, to sing the eternal praises of God."* He appeared to be resting when he opened his eyes and said, *"Good-by Dad, good-by. Oh, what a beautiful thing I see."* Dominic breathed his last. What did you see, Dominic, was it Jesus and Mary? What did Jesus say to you, when you approached the gates of Heaven, did He say, *"Enter, faithful and worthy servant; My Mother has spoken well of you. Enter, your Heavenly Family awaits you."* Pray for us and our children, Dominic Savio.

These words of Wisdom, although written thousands of years before he was born and died, belong to Dominic Savio.

"But the just man, though he die early, shall be at rest. For the age that is honorable comes not with the passing of time, nor can it be measured in terms of years. Rather understanding is the hoary crown for men, and an unsullied life, the attainment of old age. He who pleased God was loved; he lived among sinners was transported-snatched away, lest wickedness pervert his mind or deceit beguile his soul; for the witchery of paltry things obscures what is right and the whirl of desire transforms the innocent mind. Having become perfect in a short while, he reached the fullness of a long career; for his soul was pleasing to the Lord, therefore He sped him out of the

midst of wickedness. "[24]

Dominic Savio did return to the Oratory. Although his body originally was interred in the cemetery in Mondonio and later placed in a side chapel in the local church, it was later secretly brought to the Basilica of Mary, Help of Christians on the Oratory grounds in Turin, where till today, *"little Dominic"* rests, an example to all those who pass his way.

The Process to Canonization is on its way

When Cardinal Salotti,[25] then Monsignor Salotti, told Pope Pius X that he was writing a biography of Dominic Savio, the Pope told him to hurry, *"Whatever you write about Dominic Savio will be good but too little. You must work to advance his cause. Don't waste time. Push his cause speedily."* the ailing Pope, tired from too many battles fought, continued, *"Dominic Savio is a real model for the youth of our times."* When the world and the Church are in crisis, the Lord raises powerful men and women to save His Church. One Saint-Pope Pius X, who recognized the ills of the world within the Church and tried to combat them, acknowledged another Saint who was needed not only for that time, but most especially for ours. It is interesting to note that Pope Pius X and Dominic Savio were canonized the same year, one week apart.

Pope Benedict XV read Cardinal Salotti's biography of Dominic Savio and said, *"...this book is to honor a Saint who fits into our time. What I like about Dominic Savio is his gaiety, the way he was everyone's friend, and his love of fun, even the noisy kind. Our modern age no longer cares for austere penitential Saints.* "[26]

The cause of Beatification was opened in Rome with Cardinal Salotti as defender of the cause. After much study, meticulous and detailed scrutiny of his life, and lengthy careful

---

[24]Wisdom 4:7-15
[25]Much of what we have researched has come from Charles Salotti and St. Don Bosco
[26]p.161 St. Dominic Savio by St. John Bosco

deliberation, on July 9, 1933, "little Dominic" was declared *Venerable* by Pope Pius XI.

In 1950, Rome approved the two miracles, required by Church Law, which came about through the sole intercession of Dominic Savio and on March 5, 1950, Pope Pius XII solemnly declared Venerable Dominic Savio, *Blessed* in St. Peter's Basilica. This is the same year that another teen-ager, a Blessed Maria Goretti was declared a Saint.[27]

Two more miracles are required, for a Blessed to then be declared a Saint. Two more miracles were approved in 1954, both involving the instantaneous cure of mothers![28]

Late one afternoon, on a hot muggy day in June, June 12, 1954, to be exact, Pope Pius XII declared Dominic Savio a Saint of the Roman Catholic Church, extending to him all the honors of the altar. It was obvious to all that the weight of all the tragedy, of the World War he and the Church had lived through, had taken its toll on the ailing saintly Pope. But his voice belied his tired body, as he boomed out the declaration of the church welcoming this heroic, holy young man into the Glorified Ranks of the Church Triumphant - the Saints.

Dominic, taken from us before you had fully bloomed, this day Our Lord introduced you, precious, virtuous bud of God, to the world for all times, and for all generations, but most especially for this time and generation. *St. Dominic Savio, pray for us.*

You saved your mothers's life through the intercession of Our Mother Mary and the Green Scapular, saving her life and that of her unborn child, please intercede for the unborn babies who are at risk of being murdered by their mothers, who know not what they do.

Intercede for our youth of today that they might have the

---

[27]Read about her life and martyrdom in the chapter in this book: *Maria Goretti - White and Crimson Rose of Jesus.*
[28]Remember when Dominic Savio placed the green scapular on his mother and she was cured, instantaneously? Turn to p.175 for more details.

courage to desire Sainthood, and in so doing live a chaste life, that they may also receive and accept God's Grace to live like you with the motto: *"Death, but not sin!"*

St. Dominic Savio, you have made us laugh and cry as we have written your short but full life. It is finished, but you will be with us, till we face each other in Heaven. *St. Dominic Savio, save a place for us.*

Above: *St. Aloysius Gonzaga Patron of Catholic Youth*

Above: *St. Aloysius Gonzaga receives first Holy Communion*

Above: *St. Aloysius Gonzaga at two years old*

Above: *Shrine of St. Aloysius Gonzaga in Mantova, Italy*

St. Aloysius

Patron saint of Catholic Youth

St. Aloysius or Luigi Gonzaga, as he was baptized, was born on March 9, 1568, in the castle of Castiglione della Stivieri in Lombardy, Italy. St. Dominic Savio, another Saint of the young, whom we have also written about in this book, and who was called another Aloysius, *died* on March 9th, only in 1857, almost three hundred years after the birth of St. Aloysius. Coincidence or God's way of telling us something, putting the pieces of the puzzle of life together. I believe we will discover, as his story unfurls, why St. Dominic Savio was called another Aloysius.

Every time, we write a book, you ask us why this book now? As we are writing these chapters on these young Saints, God's word keeps coming to us. It's like the unreal changes of weather we have been having in this, the end of the last century of the Second Millennium. All I keep thinking, Is God talking to us, and is anyone listening? *"Speak Lord, your servant is listening."*[1]

Dominic was born into a life of poverty, of parents who were poor materially, but rich in faith. Aloysius, on the other hand, was born into a family of wealth and position. He was the oldest son of Don Ferrante, the Marquis of Castiglione and Marta Tana Santena, who as part of the royal court of Philip II of Spain, was lady of honor to the Queen. Not only did his mother have a highly esteemed honor, his father held a prestigious position in the court, as well. So, baby Luigi (Aloysius) was born into the velvets and purples of his century.

Now, it is noteworthy to mention that he was also born of a people who had resisted the holocaust of Lutheranism and Calvinism that had spread to the northern parts of Europe, swallowing up whole nations. The Spaniards held fast to their Faith. After almost seven hundred years of domination by the

---

[1] 1 Samuel 3:9

Moors, when uttering the Name of Jesus and worshiping in the Catholic Church was punishable by death, the Catholic Queen Isabela determined, never again would her fair land be lost to Jesus and His Church. When the Church was again threatened, Isabela's loyal sons would carry on for her and block the enemy from entering her land and conquering the souls of the faithful. She had claimed them for Jesus and Spain, a land of soldiers and poets, and she fought to keep Spain for Jesus and His Church.

When Ferrante's first-born son came into the world, like most fathers, he had a dream and a plan for Luigi; he was to be a great soldier. His son would fulfill his father's dream for him, but as *a soldier of Christ*. Ferrante began executing his plan for his son, at age four, starting him off with a miniature battlefield, equipped with a set of tiny soldiers, scale model guns and all forms of battle regalia, all in minuscule dimensions.

A year later, at five years old, his father took him to Casalmaggiore, where three thousand men were being trained to join a Spanish expedition which would attack Tunis (or Tunisia). The little boy of five was enthralled with all the parades and the life-size soldiers practicing real life maneuvers; it was like a huge playground, and he was playing with the big guys. The months spent there were like a dream come true for a little boy. He was allowed to join the *big soldiers*, marching in the parades, often up in the front of a platoon. He was a sight to behold; they had outfitted him with a long wooden spear sporting a metal arrowhead, which he carried slung over his tiny shoulder. The spear, at least four times his size, trailed behind him, as he jaunted proudly trying to keep in step with the others.

Luigi was a typical little boy, left on his own, open to mischief and trouble. One day, he picked up a gun which someone had carelessly left around for a little person to find and... Well, the opportunity presenting itself, without any assistance, except his own resourcefulness, he loaded the musket with ammunition and fired it off while the entire camp was resting. After they were sure he was unharmed, they were not very happy campers or soldiers.

His father had wanted him to be a soldier, well he was sure learning; but I don't think it was what his father had in mind, when he brought him there. Hanging around the soldiers, he almost became part of the woodwork and they hardly noticed him listening to their flowery language. He learned a vocabulary which was not in keeping with a gentleman and future knight. When he returned home, he innocently repeated the colorful but coarse language he had picked up. Needless to say, his tutor was not very happy. He was careful to explain that such language was not only scandalous but blasphemous and made Jesus most unhappy. Little Luigi, head downcast, was deeply remorseful, tears spilling from his eyes, at the thought he had wounded Jesus. Even years later, he sorrowed over the sin which he had so grievously committed.

At age seven, Luigi was to have the *Hounds of Heaven* begin to pursue him. Although he began saying morning and evening prayers from the time he was just a baby, his spirituality was to accelerate when at age seven he began reciting the Office of Our Lady, the seven penitential psalms, and other devotions. He could be seen praying on his knees on the bare stone floor, without the comfort of even a cushion. Luigi had completely, unconditionally surrendered his life to God, so much so that his spiritual director, St. Robert Bellarmine, as well as his other confessors, said that in their opinion, Aloysius (Luigi) never committed a mortal sin, in his lifetime.

Aloysius goes to Tuscany

In 1577, when Aloysius was nine years old, his father took him and his brother Ridolfo to Florence, Italy. He left them with tutors, who were to help the boys improve their Latin and learn how to speak the Italian of Tuscany, which was considered the *proper* Italian of the aristocracy. From his later writings, we never see a glimpse of the progress Aloysius made in the sciences of the world, but when he expressed his love for Florence, calling the city *"the mother of piety,"* he clearly showed the strides he made there in the sciences of the Saints. God was again forming a young boy into a spotless vessel, introducing him to the lives of the great Tuscan Saints Catherine and Bernardine of Siena, to mention a few.

Florence has always been a city of great contrasts, as Aloysius would soon discover. His station, as son of a nobleman, required he appear at the grand duke's court, frequently. There he saw the seamier side of Florence, a civilization polluted by deceit, an unquenchable thirst for power, all-consuming greed, which stopped at nothing to fill its gluttonous desires. Poison, fraud, licentious behavior, perversion of all kinds permeated the court. Rather than lead the young nobleman Aloysius into a life of decadence and self-will, he became more and more aware it was the devil's handiwork, and it caused him to more ardently desire a chaste, virtuous life.

He protected not only *his* soul, but the cherished souls of his companions, sharing with them spiritual exercises and disciplines reminiscent of the early desert fathers. We can see the Hand of the Lord, again in the life of Aloysius, as this could not be the ordinary response of a nine year old boy. That the Lord is bestowing upon him, extraordinary Grace is evident; but the Lord having won his heart, the boy is *cooperating* with that Grace. They said of him that he would avert temptation, shielding his eyes and soul from the women of the court, keeping his eyes lowered in their presence. Modesty was his vanguard, allowing no one to see any part of his body, concealing it from even his valet; not the smallest toe on one of his feet would he bare.

Aloysius leaves one court, only to be placed in another.

A little more than two years passed, when Aloysius and his brother had to move once again. Their father, in response to the Duke of Mantua making him governor of Monserrat, brought his two sons to Mantua to serve in the duke's court. It was November, 1579 and Aloysius was eleven years and eight months old. This move was exceedingly painful for him, and counterproductive to boot. Aloysius had already decided to relinquish his right, as the eldest son, to the title of Marquis of Castiglione, to his younger brother Ridolfo. He had this plan, in spite of the fact that he, Aloysius had already been commissioned by the emperor to succeed his father, after his death, as Marquis.

Aloysius was in a difficult situation; it was required he take his place, as heir-apparent, to make appearances in the Court. God to the rescue! Aloysius was debilitated by an extremely excruciating attack, due to a diseased kidney, and had to curtail his activities! Now confined to his quarters, doctor's orders, we find Aloysius earnestly devouring stories of the Saints and when not reading, praying. This illness left him so incapacitated, it so affected his digestive system, he was incapable of eating and ingesting most food

Aloysius had an unquenchable thirst to learn about the Faith and the history of the Church. Again, we see the merciful God coming to the aid of His Church. His Church was under attack, with Luther and Calvin, trying their darnedest to lead the faithful away from their Church. God raised up a Saint in the most unlikely of places, in the midst of a decadent society - checks and balances. Aloysius became interested in the Jesuits. One of the books he had been reading told of the evangelization that brave Jesuit missionaries were doing in India. This burned Aloysius' heart! He could think of nothing but becoming a Jesuit missionary, leaving for India and working toward the conversion of the unbelievers to Jesus and the Catholic Church.

So few of us do anything, waiting for what we believe the Lord is calling us to do, that ministry we want to join or better yet start, we end up dying, never having served the Lord, at all. Not so, with Aloysius! What better way to bring the Treasures of the Church to the souls in India, begin by teaching Catechism to the poor children of Castiglione! And this is how he spent his summer months, and holidays, waiting upon the Lord to send him to India.

Summer over, Aloysius would spend his winters in Casale-

Above:
St. Aloysius Gonzaga teaching the children about Heaven.

Above: *St. Aloysius Gonzaga practiced the ascetic life of a monk, he would rise at midnight and pray on the stone floor.*

Above:
Death of St. Aloysius Gonzaga He died during the Octave of the Feast of Corpus Christi.

Right:
The skull of St. Aloysius Gonzaga in his Shrine in Mantova, Italy

Monferrato, going from one church to another, borrowing
spirituality from the Capuchins and then from the Barnabites. He
began to practice the ascetic life of a monk; he fasted three times
a week solely on bread and water; he flagellated himself with a
whip; he would rise at midnight and pray on the stone floor.
Now, if you ever have the opportunity to visit an ancient
monastery or castle, even in the heated days of summer, the
rooms are cold and dank; Aloysius would not permit a fire to
warm his room, no matter how cold it was.

[He reminds me of us, when we began our Journey of
Faith. Having just returned to the Church, we couldn't get
enough; we were spiritual hogs devouring every morsel of
spiritual food, seeking all the Treasures of the Church, spending
every free moment we could muster, every vacation - going to
Europe, pilgrimaging to places where the Saints lived and died,
following their lives and their spirituality. I guess our hunger has
not been satisfied; we're still reading, studying and journeying.
And so it was with Aloysius. I guess, we like him, allowed the
hounds of Heaven to catch up to us and capture our hearts.]

Two years have passed; it is time for Aloysius to move on.

It is 1581, and Don Ferrante, Aloysius' father, is called by
the Crown to accompany the Empress Maria of Austria on her
trip from Bohemia to Spain. He took his entire family with him.
When they arrived in Spain, Aloysius had to face another crisis;
he and brother Ridolfo were selected to serve as pages to Don
Diego, Prince of Asturias. Although his heart was elsewhere, out
of obedience to his father and loyalty to the Emperor, Aloysius
tirelessly cared for the young Prince, helping him with his
studies, and patiently waiting on him, addressing his every whim.

His faithful allegiance to his appointed task did not take
away from Aloysius' commitment to saying his prayers. His
usual spiritual exercises entailed hours; Aloysius had to be
satisfied with the menial hour available to him for his daily
meditation. But to meditate one hour without distraction, which
was his goal, required *hours* of soulful preparation. Because of

this, he appeared solemn and introspective; his mind seemed to be elsewhere (which it was). The other members of the court began to whisper about Aloysius. They started to make fun of him, saying he wasn't human; and if he was, he was not quite all there!

Aloysius knew it was time to break it to his parents that he desired to become a Jesuit. He thought it best to tell his mother; then she could tactfully discuss it with his father. He had no problem with his mother who immediately gave her consent. Now, it was time for his father. His mother Marta barely finished her sentence when Don Ferrante blew! He was livid! His temper overriding his good judgment, he fumed, he ranted, he raved and then he threatened to have Aloysius whipped. It was hard for him to understand why a young man of privilege with a promising career ahead of him, wanted to give it all up to become a missionary.

As he had lost large sums of money, he suspected his wife was telling him this, to coerce him into giving up gambling. However, friends of his at court, who had noticed Aloysius' reserved prayerful demeanor, convinced Don Ferrante of the boy's sincerity. His father reluctantly gave his consent, on the provision he would wait until his obligation at the court was completed. It was obvious Don Ferrante was playing for time, but time was to run out, the young Prince died! The two brothers were released from their duties. Their two year stay in Spain over, the family left for Italy, July, 1584. Aloysius was now sixteen years old.

The battle not over - Aloysius faces additional opposition

Upon the family arriving in Italy, they went directly to their estate in Castiglione and the war resumed on another front; Italy was not about to bring Aloysius any more relief than he'd had at court in Spain. His relatives, including the Duke of Mantua, all joined in, siding with his father, to oppose vehemently the young Aloysius' aspirations to become a Jesuit. They called in reinforcements. Prominent clergy and distinguished laity took turns arguing, then pleading; cajoling, then attacking; reasoning turned into threat making, all to no avail. Aloysius was resolute in his desire to become a Jesuit!

Don Ferrante left no stone unturned; he was fighting for what he felt was his son's best interest. Ferrante's god was one of position and power, how could he understand his son's God Who chose to be born of little estate and die for the sins of the world? A new plan! Send Aloysius to all the kings of northern Italy. Italy was composed of twenty-seven small kingdoms or principalities, each with its own sovereign. His father was sure this would change Aloysius' mind. That failing, he insisted he accept different secular positions. Surely that would pique his interest and he would forget the whole foolish idea. At least it would forestall the inevitable. But to his father's consternation, Aloysius was not moved; rather he was more adamant than ever, to follow his star to Jesus through joining the Jesuits.

The journey begins; Aloysius is on his way

Each day was filled with hope, only to end with disappointment. One day, his father would give his consent; the next day he would take it back. This went on and on, until the emperor sent a delegation with his edict that the rite of succession to the seat of the Marquis of Castiglione had been transferred to Aloysius' brother Ridolfo. Finally realizing all opposition was futile, his father gave his consent. At last, his parents having blessed him, Aloysius departed for Rome and his dream.

On November 25, 1585, Aloysius now eighteen years old, at last entered the *Jesuit Novitiate House of Sant' Andrea.* Settled in his tiny cell, he could be heard ecstatically exclaiming, *"This is my rest forever and ever; here I dwell, for I have chosen it."* Six weeks passed when his joy was turned to grief mixed with bliss. His father died, but not before having completely turned his life around; he called for a priest and was given the Last Rites of the Church. His eldest son had relinquished all rights to fame and position, acclaim in this world, for service to

His Heavenly King and life eternal in His Heavenly Kingdom. Aloysius had refused a golden crown on earth and God gave him the most precious crown adorned with priceless stones and diamonds, the souls (including his father's) saved through his sacrifice and example.

[In the ministry, we have found that every time we are called to sacrifice, the Lord blesses us equal to, if not more than the magnitude of the sacrifice.]

The sign of a Saint is not the gifts bestowed upon him: gifts like bilocation, ecstasy, the stigmata, reading men's souls, heavenly fragrance and others; they are simply gifts from the Lord. It is the living out of a virtuous life, in keeping with one's vocation. One of the greatest signs of sainthood is *obedience*! You will find it in the lives of all the Saints.

Aloysius' biographers say that there is not much known about how he spent the two years following his entrance into the Novitiate, except, *and that's a big except*, he obeyed, even when he found it a hardship. His superiors were keenly aware of his frail health. In an attempt to strengthen him, and restore him to good health, they required that he have some sort of recreation. He was to curb his fasting and eat more than he had at home. And most trying of all, he was to try to think of things which would divert his attention from the deeply spiritual. They hoped, in this way to prevent him from going into ecstasy. He was forbidden to pray or meditate, except at designated times. This act of obedience, training his mind to refrain from dwelling on the Treasures of Heaven, was the most difficult for Aloysius; his heart was already there, his eyes focused on what lay ahead for him with the Father.

Now, think about it; he joined the Novitiate to live a life centered on the Lord and future life with Him, and he has to limit his thinking of Him? It doesn't sound logical. It is *super logical* or Divine. By this sacrifice, was God asking him to be there to do *His Will*, and to die to Aloysius' will? How would Aloysius know his Father's Will? Obey his superiors, even when he was not in agreement, especially when he was not in agreement. In studying the lives of the Saints, we find God telling them that by obeying their superiors they were doing His Will.

[When someone applies for entrance into the ministry, we ask why they want to enter. If they say they have come because they want to do God's Will, we can be pretty sure they will stay. If instead, they have a pre-existing notion or agenda, the Lord will blow them out of the ministry.]

Aloysius made every action a prayer! Coming from the aristocracy, he was fully aware he was not proficient in physical labor of any kind. He had been trained to be a knight, not a peasant. But this is what he chose to do! The more humble the assignment, the more subservient the job, the more physically and demeaning the work, the happier he was. As with Saints Anthony of Padua and Teresa of Avila, he found God among the pots and pans; he loved to work in the kitchen washing dishes and cleaning up after others around the novitiate. He genuinely performed all the servile duties allowed him, with excitement. What the world judged menial, he found meaningful.

He was at a Novitiate in Milan, when one day, as he was praying, he had a vision revealing he would not be on earth much longer. This filled his Heart with unfathomable joy, and from that time he had only one vision, to prepare for things *Above*, not below. He more and more separated himself from the distractions of the world. His superiors saw his health getting progressively worse, his strength ebbing out of him, draining him. The weather in Milan tended to be harsh in the winter. In Rome, the climate was temperate, and consequently more agreeable to his health.

It was decided that Aloysius would go to Rome to complete his studies in Theology. Upon arrival, he managed to choose the most austere niche in the house, a room in the attic. A tiny window in the roof of his room provided the only light, which at rare intervals cut through the darkness, to brighten his little cubby hole. His simple furnishings consisted of a bed, one chair and a stool upon which he placed his books. But to him, this was more splendid than the most magnificently adorned room in the palaces where he had lived. Here, he and the Lord could communicate, undisturbed.

The other seminarians commented they could see him deeply absorbed, meditating. He seemed oblivious of his surroundings at school, and when walking in the corridors of the cloister. He would become so deeply contemplative, he would often be seen going into ecstasy at the most unlikely places, at the most unlikely times. It could be at dinner, or during his strictly prescribed recreation time. Lost in prayer, unaware of his surroundings, the noise, the other students, he would be deeply immersed in some sort of dialogue with another People in another World, ecstasy. Even when the other seminarians called to him, shouting that recreation time was over and they had to go back to class, he did not acknowledge them.

He was restricted to the amount of time he could spend contemplating God (as it would bring him into a state of ecstasy and further weaken his health). Whatever time he did have was so filled with *unsurpassable joy*, he so longed to be united with Jesus in Heaven, he would get lost in ecstasy. As with other Saints, just the *thought* of the Lord, the mere *mention* of His Name, would lead him to contemplate on the Lord he would be with someday, the One he would behold in His Beatific Vision, and that was enough to have him go into ecstasy. His superiors tried to restrain him from weakening himself, but all they could do was pray for this little future Saint, in their midst, that the Lord would keep him with them a little longer.

It was 1591. Luther and Calvin had swept Europe with their heresies, cutting away at the very heart of the faithful, causing division. Mankind, confused, started to turn away from God. A plague broke out. An epidemic spread until it reached and ravaged Rome. No one was excused from its tentacles of pain and misery, the dead piling high in the streets, with barely enough well people who would dare take them away. Loved ones, often frightened of catching the dreaded disease, left the ill to die, uncared for, alone. The Jesuits opened a hospital to tend the sick. With the Father General leading the way, other Jesuits risked their lives, as they spent every waking moment giving solace and comfort to the sick and the Sacraments to the dying. Aloysius begged to join his brothers and was reluctantly given permission to work alongside his fellow Jesuits.

He went among the ill, bathing them with love and compassion. An angel of mercy, he was very often responsible for bringing them closer to Jesus, preparing them to meet their Savior. He tended them, placing cold cloths on their feverish foreheads, cleaning them, gently washing their pain-wracked bodies. He made their beds, cleaned out their bed pans. No job too menial, too trivial, to him they were Jesus and he had an opportunity to soothe Jesus' Wounds, as he could not while He was alive. In this way, by soothing their wounds, these *"the least of His children,"* he was in his small way soothing the Wounds of his Lord. As was expected, the Jesuit priests, aiding the sick and dying, also fell victims to the plague and Aloysius nursing them, caught the death-threatening disease.

Aloysius, believing that this was the end and he was dying, was filled with joy. This was what the prophecy meant; this was how and when he was to die; he was soon to be with his Jesus! Anxious to be on his way, he received his Viaticum and was anointed. His delight was all too premature. To the amazement of everyone, especially his own, he recovered. But the epidemic left its scars; a low fever further crippled him; he was reduced to an invalid barely able to lift his head. He went from bad to worse. Three months after having been afflicted, he was confined to his bed. At night, when he could muster enough strength, he would rise from bed, and he would worship his Lord on the Crucifix. He would painfully shuffle from holy picture to holy picture, kissing our Blessed Mother, all the Angels and the Saints depicted. Then, braced between the bed and wall, he knelt and prayed, for as long as his strength held up.

Paradise his dream, he humbly asked his confessor and spiritual director, if it was possible that anyone could go directly to God in Heaven, without passing through Purgatory.[2]   St. Robert Bellarmine assured him it was not only possible, but knowing him the way that he did, it was altogether feasible that he, Aloysius would receive that Grace from God.   With that, Aloysius fell into a deep ecstasy that lasted through the night.   It was during this ecstasy, he was to learn that he would die on the octave of Corpus Christi, the Feast Day of the Body and Blood of Christ, Jesus in the Eucharist Whom he so passionately loved. On each of the eight days Aloysius would intone the *Te Deum*, in thanksgiving to the Lord for deeming it His Will that Aloysius would soon see Him.

Those with him, would at times hear him recite, *"I rejoiced when they said to me: We will go into the house of the Lord."*[3] At other times, he would say, *"We are going, gladly, gladly!"* On the eighth day of the octave, he looked so much better, they spoke of sending him to the town of Frascati.   But to their dismay, he pleaded to receive Viaticum, as he tried to make them understand he would die before the morning sun.   They reluctantly complied with his wishes.   When his provincial came into his room to see how he was doing, Aloysius joyfully greeted him with, *"We are going, Father; we are going."*   To which the provincial asked, *"Where?"*   Aloysius replied, *"To Heaven."*   The provincial, seeing the great improvement in Aloysius said, *"Listen to the young man.   He speaks of going to Heaven, as we speak of going to Frascati."*

Evening came.   As Aloysius was looking so well and definitely out of danger, they left him with just a couple of Jesuits to watch over him.   All the rest were relieved of their watch and sent to bed.   But at Aloysius' insistence, St. Robert Bellarmine intoned the prayers for the dying.   The little soldier of Christ lay still, breaking the silence with his occasional whispering, *"Into*

[2]Read *Visions of Heaven, Hell and Purgatory* by Bob and Penny Lord
[3]Psalm 122:1

Thy Hands." No one believed he was dying, until he suddenly turned for the worse. It was between eleven and twelve o'clock at night, when they noticed his labored breathing. He began to sink deeper and deeper into the World he so often spoke of. His earthly strength giving out to new promise and Heavenly power, he began to breath his last. His eyes fixed on the Crucifix he so loved, he called out *Jesus,* and at midnight the evening of June the 20th, the boy who traded the riches of this world for those of the next, went *Home!* He was twenty-three years old.

The relics of St. Aloysius lie under the altar in the Lancelotti Chapel of the Church of St. Ignatius in Rome, where they can still be venerated. Miracles began to happen immediately. In so short a time, the virtue and piety, the holiness of this young man who lived his life with an eye on eternity, spread to all parts of Italy, the rest of Europe and then across the sea to the United States. Living a *holy life* on earth, he received the key to *eternal life* with his Savior. A word to the young and the not-so-young, *Pray to St. Aloysius for purity. He will bring you to Sainthood.*

He was proclaimed a *Saint* by Benedict XIII, on December 31, 1726. He was named *Protector of Catholic students* of the entire world, November 22, 1729. And in 1926, Pope Pius XI declared him *Patron Saint of the youth of the World.*

We are in the days of great Saints and deadly sinners. Live your life with your eyes on Jesus and He will lead you to Sainthood and *Home!* Cast your lot with the enemy of God with his false, fleeting promises and he will not only betray you on earth, he will drag you down with him to the bowels of hell. Saints like St. Aloysius made a choice in life, while very young. He chose the crown awaiting him in Heaven rather than the temporary crown on earth which will tarnish. Look in the mirror! What do you see? Is that the one you want to stand before Our precious Lord, Who loved you so much, when asked, *"How much do you love me?"* opened His Arms wide on the Cross and said, *"This much."* We love you! You can be a Saint!

Left: ***Statue of St. Stanislaus Kostka in the Gesu, Rome St. Stanislaus Kostka was born in Poland in the royal castle of Rostkovo in 1550.***

Right:
St. Stanislaus Kostka receives the Eucharist from an Angel

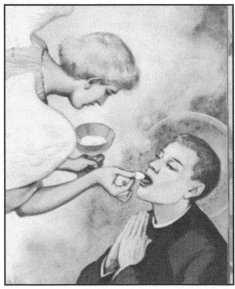

St. Stanislaus Kostka

Patron Saint of Polish Youth

Penny and I believe that when we were born, part of our hearts remained in Heaven in the Lord's safekeeping, waiting to be reunited with us. To quote St. Augustine, a powerful Doctor and early Father of the Church, *"My heart is restless until it rests in Thee, O Lord."* For some, that restlessness to be with Jesus in the Kingdom remains with us all our life, from the day we come out of our mother's womb until the day we are placed in the tomb. It can take the form of a dull ache or a sharp, roaring, pounding, searing pain. We can see and sense how certain of God's people with whom we come in contact, are in constant communication with the Almighty. Such was the case with St. Joseph of Cupertino, whom many accused of being backward or retarded, both of which he was neither; he was just not there! When he was in communication with our Heavenly Family, he was in a different place, somewhere else, in Heaven with Our Lord Jesus and Our Mother Mary. Perhaps he was supposed to be putting dishes away at a Monastery at this given time; he could not be blamed if he knocked things over or dropped them; he was off with Jesus and Mary.

We can sense that some people we meet in our lives are *Saints in progress* waiting impatiently to finish their journey on earth. We have read the words of Saints who consider themselves foreigners in this land, pilgrims just passing through, on the way to Heaven, anxious to get on with it. Perhaps that is why a Dominic Savio at fifteen years old, a Maria Goretti at twelve years old, a Rose of Viterbo at fifteen years old, is ready to enter the Kingdom. Perhaps that's why a Stanislaus Kostka was ready from the day he was born to go *Home* to be united with his Heavenly family, and at age seventeen, was becoming really anxious. The Roman Martyrology states that *"he was made perfect in a short while and fulfilled many times by the*

Angelic innocence of his life."[1] We wonder if it was that, or was it that he never quite put both feet on the earth; one foot was always in Heaven, waiting for the rest of him to join it.

The Lord puts His special people in the most unexpected situations, and then contradicts the standards of the world. St. Stanislaus Kostka represents many things to the people of God. While he is not considered a victim of the Protestant Reformation, his life was terribly affected by Protestants and the aftermath of the Reformation. He was placed in a noble family of Poland, son of a prominent man, a senator. He had an older brother who loved all the things Stanislaus detested. This brother was interested in anything which would amuse him, entertain him, gratify his senses, and he wanted nothing to do with *anything* that would cause him to sacrifice or do without the pleasures of the world, for even a moment. It's so hard to believe that the two, Paul Kostka and Stanislaus Kostka came from the same family. It's like one was a virgin birth, or born of a different set of parents and then kidnapped by pirates and ransomed to this family. We can accept anything but that the two, Paul and Stanislaus, were blood brothers. And yet that's God's contradiction. Paul might have been put on the earth to be Stanislaus' means of flagellation, while Stanislaus may have been meant to be the source of Paul's conversion.

Stanislaus was born in Poland, in the royal castle of Rostkovo in 1550, four years after Martin Luther died. It was obvious to all, very early in his life that he was not like anyone else in the family, least of all his father and brother. He showed a great deal of interest in prayers, matters of Church, spiritual exercises, and studying. He shied away from tasteless and indecent talk. His father was almost embarrassed by Stanislaus' behavior, or at least his *prudish tendencies*. He would say to guests in the home, "Don't tell that story before Stanislaus. He

---

[1]Butler's Lives of the Saints Vol IV - Pg 335

would faint."[2] While he was not reprimanding Stanislaus for his virtuous decorum, he was sort of apologizing for the fact that he might not have been considered a *real man* to some of those present.

We're not told of his relationship with his mother at all. But we would have to believe that he received a great deal of his spirituality from that dear, saintly woman. Someone had to take credit for this beautiful manifestation of God's glory that was Stanislaus Kostka. It surely wasn't his father or his brother.

There's nothing known for sure about Stanislaus in his early life. The first the biographers hear of him is when he moved with his brother and a tutor to Vienna, to be close to his studies at the Jesuit College. Here they were, Jekyl and Hyde, from the same family. It had to be a contradiction for the people who met them, one being the image of Sanctity, and the other, well....The boys were tutored by a Dr. John Bilinsky, who had tutored them at home in Poland. Dr. Bilinsky traveled with them to Vienna, and continued to tutor them privately.

They stayed at the Jesuit college for the first eight months in Vienna, and then because the Emperor Maxmilian took the houses away from the Jesuits, brother Paul used this as an excuse to intimidate their tutor, Dr. Bilinsky, who must have been their chaperone as well, to move them into a very secular, high class apartment which was more likely in the style to which they were accustomed back home in Poland. There was only one problem; the owner of the apartment they had rented, was a very zealous Lutheran, and he ran a strict Lutheran house.

There's no indication that this caused a problem as long as the boys did not try to bring their religious beliefs home with them from school. Well, that was definitely not a problem for Paul, because as far as we have been able to determine, he either had no religious beliefs or he just didn't practice any. But there may have been tension between the landlord and young fourteen

---

[2]Butler's Lives of the Saints Vol IV - Pg 335

year old Stanislaus, who could not help but exude his love for Jesus, Mary, the Angels and Saints through the Catholic Church. I mean, he was Church with a capital "C." But the Angels must have been protecting Stanislaus, because he did all his praying and devotions in his room when he was not at college or church. He was a very quiet young man, however, and the landlord most likely never heard him.

He also practiced mortifications, which meant he scourged his body with a small wire whip, or wore a rough hair shirt or something in that nature. He was determined that desires of the flesh would not rule his life. He did not want to take a chance on falling victim to anything that could possibly jeopardize his relationship with Jesus and the Holy Family of Mary, Angels and Saints. It's not so much that he was fearful of imperiling his soul, which we're sure he was, but he was more concerned about hurting Jesus, or separating himself from this relationship he had developed with the Holy Family. He felt a part of a huge family, a community of loving Relatives who would never leave him or hurt him. It would have to be *he* who would take the first step in alienating himself from the family of God. And he knew that while he might do that, they would still love him and long for him to return. But he did not want to hurt them, or make them yearn for his return; he never wanted to leave them.

Stanislaus had a great love, devotion and respect for the Real Presence of Jesus in the Eucharist. This was not a time in the Church when you could receive daily, but if it had been allowed, he would most likely have been among the first to receive his Lord on a daily basis. He would fast for an entire day prior to receiving the Eucharist. Jesus in the Eucharist was his entire life. He knew without a doubt that reception of the Eucharist was *physically* as well as *spiritually* nourishing. A time would come when this would be put to the test. After a little less than two years living in this apartment, Stanislaus became very ill. He thought he was dying. He was *sure* he was dying. He wanted a priest to come to the apartment to give him

Viaticum.[3] The Lutheran landlord refused to allow a priest to enter his house. We believe Paul and Dr. Bilinsky did all they could to change the mind of the Lutheran landlord, but to no avail. Paul tried to keep from Stanislaus the fact that the landlord would not allow the priest into the house. He kept insisting Stanislaus was not really that sick, in the hopes that he and the chaperone, Dr. Bilinsky, would be able to wear the Lutheran down. This was not happening.

Stanislaus was sure he was on death's door. He had belonged to a sodality of St. Barbara, who is a defender of the Eucharist and a very strong Saint in our Church. He appealed to her, praying to her to put herself in the presence of Jesus, and ask Him to intercede for him, and allow the Eucharist to be brought to him. He prayed for all he was worth. He could feel the perspiration pouring down from his head. He knew he was praying for his life. He felt a presence in the room. A coolness came over him as if a soft breeze from Heaven had entered the room. It might have been from the movement of the wings of Angels, because he saw before him two Angels with St. Barbara[4] in between them. She was carrying the Eucharist in a Heavenly ciborium. As they approached him, he thought his heart would surely burst. The Angels administered the Sacrament of the Eucharist to Stanislaus. He could feel their closeness to him. They radiated a warmth and fragrance which he had never experienced before. They stayed with him for a short time, joining him as he offered Thanksgiving to the Lord for giving him this miracle. St. Barbara looked at him affectionately. She never said a word to him with her lips, but her eyes told him so much. They showed a tremendous love for him. Then St. Barbara and the Angels left.

---

[3]Viaticum-our last Holy Communion, part of the *Last Rites* of the Church, given to someone critically ill, near death. Today the Sacrament is called the *Blessing of the Sick*, but in those days it was called *Extreme Unction*.
[4]St. Barbara is known to be the protectress of persons in danger of dying without receiving the Last Sacraments.

St. Stanislaus lay in his room peacefully after this miraculous visit from his Heavenly Family, affirming that they would always be there to guide him and protect him, to keep him from all evil. He could feel the peace of the presence of Our Lord Jesus inside him. The perspiration left his body; his breathing became more natural; a feeling of calm enveloped him. He was happier than he had ever been. But his joy was to be *magnified*, when he was next given a gift so great his heart almost burst. *Our Lady appeared to him holding the Child Jesus.* She serenely placed Jesus in the arms of this fifteen year-old boy. Stanislaus could feel his heart pounding as if it would come out of his body. His eyes could not fully behold the dazzling beauty of the vision of Mary before him. He had never seen anyone as radiant, as regal, as serene, as loving, as she in his life. He could not even begin to describe her; she was from another dimension beyond description. All the most exquisite art he had ever seen paled, in the illustrious presence of the Mother of God, Mary most holy. He thought he would die of ecstasy, and he was looking forward to it. Mary spoke to his heart. She told him many things that day, mostly for him and for the life he would lead in glorifying the Lord through his example, but one message she gave him that we know of, is he was to enter into the Society of Jesus, the Jesuit community.

When Our Lady first recommended the Jesuits to Stanislaus, his heart skipped a beat. He had wanted to join that order, but had not had the courage to go forward with his desire. She gave him the affirmation and push he needed to catapult him into action. This sounded like a simple demand from the Mother of God, but it would not be simple to execute. Stanislaus came from a powerful Polish family. No one wanted to incur the wrath of his father. So when Stanislaus approached the Jesuit provincial in Vienna, although the man would like to have had Stanislaus for many reasons, he insisted that the young man get his parents' permission before entering into the community.

Both Stanislaus and the provincial knew this was not going

to happen. Stanislaus asked the advice of another Jesuit, who suggested he present himself to the head of the Society of Jesus in Germany. So, on his own, Stanislaus began his journey to Augsburg, some 450 miles away, to appeal to a higher court, St. Peter Canisius, who was the provincial in Upper Germany. He began his adventure on August 10, 1567. He was just under seventeen years old. For some reason, perhaps financial, Stanislaus decided to walk this great distance. But he knew his dreaded brother Paul and most likely the chaperone, Dr. Bilinsky, would be after him in short order, so he decided on a disguise. Once outside of Vienna, he spied a pilgrim, dressed in very harsh clothing, not at all what Stanislaus or anyone of his class would be caught dead wearing. Perhaps for that reason, when the brother and Dr. Bilinsky went in search of Stanislaus, they passed him on the road without even recognizing him, so good was his disguise. They continued on the road. When they didn't see him anywhere, they assumed he had gone a different way.

It was just Stanislaus' luck, or was it the Lord making him really work for this vocation, that when he arrived at Augsburg, St. Peter was not there, but another day's journey away, off in Dillingen. But that didn't stop our hero. It might have slowed him down somewhat, because he had truly thought the end would be in Augsburg. When he was given the additional task of going one more day's journey, it was not what he would have wanted; but he offered it up and continued on his way. He reminds us a lot of another zealot we have written about, St. Louis Marie de Montfort, who walked from Poitiers, France, to Rome and back, in an effort to have the Pope tell him what his ministry should be. Well, this young man was doing basically the same.

When Stanislaus finally arrived at Dillingen, he went to St. Peter Canisius and fell to his knees. He offered himself to St. Peter, giving him a letter of recommendation from the same Jesuit who had recommended he travel to Germany to see the provincial. St. Peter could very easily see the simplicity of the young man. He immediately accepted him into the Society. As a test of Stanislaus' resolve, St. Peter put him to work at menial tasks, waiting on other students and cleaning their rooms. This was a great trial for Stanislaus, coming from nobility, and most likely, never having had to do any of the work St. Peter required of him. The future Saint threw himself into the task, with great humility and respect for the Jesuit students. He did so well the students were overwhelmed by his behavior, but completely impressed. Who knows, Stanislaus may have been an example for them in their training as future disciples of St. Ignatius of Loyola, their father-in-faith.

Stanislaus feared this was not a good place for him to be, as it was too close to his brother and Dr. Bilinsky, and within reach of his father, who would not be long in coming after him. You must realize that they didn't consider being a religious a suitable vocation for Stanislaus, much less that of a Jesuit, whose order, the father was not really in love with. St. Peter Canisius agreed it was not prudent or safe for Stanislaus to remain; and within a short time, Stanislaus was sent to Rome where he was officially accepted into the order by St. Francis Borgia, who was the Superior General of the Society of Jesus. He couldn't go any higher than that. Nor could his father appeal to anyone higher than St. Francis, other than the Pope himself. When St. Peter Canisius sent Stanislaus, he also sent a letter to his superior, St. Francis Borgia. It went like this:

"He is a Polish noble and his name is Stanislaus. He is an excellent, intelligent young man....On his arrival here he was so eager to carry out his long-standing ambition - some years ago he committed himself unreservedly to the Society, though not yet admitted to it....He was very eager to be sent to Rome to be as far away as possible from any harassment by his family. He also wished to advance as much as he could in the path of holiness....We hope for great things from him."[5]

---

[5]Jesuit Saints & Martyrs - Joseph N. Tylenda SJ Pg 403

St. Francis Borgia accepted Stanislaus into the community in 1567, at seventeen years old. We're not sure if St. Francis Borgia had ever run into a situation like this before, being only the third Superior General of the Society of Jesus, or if he was fully aware of the possible ramifications his actions might cause him or the Society. But whatever could happen did happen. The barrage of complaints and threats began weaving their way from Poland (Stanislaus' father) to Rome. He accused St. Francis and the Jesuits of abusing his son by forcing him to wear "contemptible dress and following a profession unworthy of his birth." He threatened to have the Jesuits banished from Poland. Stanislaus was given the chore of answering his father, which he did in a most respectful manner, but also very firm. He had not gone through the rough times walking all the way to Rome to buckle under the pressure of his father, or his brother or Dr. Bilinsky for that matter. The pressure lessened but never subsided and shortly after the death of our Saint, his brother Paul came out of the woodwork. But we'll get to that part later.

He was given the ultimate gift of spending three months at the Jesuit residence at the Gesù in Rome. For an outsider, that may not mean much. But for those of us who have been given the privilege to walk through the magnificent church of the Gesù, and visit the living quarters of the hero of the Jesuits, their father-in-faith, and one of the most powerful men of this time,[6] it was an awesome experience we will never forget.[7] Keep in mind that St.

---

[6]Read a full account of the life of St. Ignatius of Loyola in Bob and Penny Lord's book, Super Saints Book III - *Defenders of the Faith - Saints of the Counter-Reformation*

[7]*[Author's note: We visited the church of the Gesù this last summer, as well as the residence of St. Ignatius. We did a lot of videotaping there for a television program on St. Ignatius which is part of our series, Super Saints, for EWTN. He has been dead over 450 years, and his Society has experienced many changes, and yet the spirit of St. Ignatius can still be felt in this place.]*

Ignatius had only died eleven years before this young man hallowed these halls. His spirit could still be felt there.

St. Stanislaus spent another month at the Roman College, and his last months of his novitiate at St. Andrew's at Quirinale. It was a very short novitiate, only ten months, after which he gave his life to Our Lord Jesus. But it may have been the most intense course of spiritual growth and pure prayer life that anyone has ever experienced. He had such a great love for the Church, for the Mass, for the Eucharist, he would become flushed the minute he walked into Church for Mass. During thanksgiving after having received Our Lord Jesus in the Eucharist, he often went into ecstasy. The Eucharist was the most important part of his life. He waited *excitedly* to receive the Lord whenever he was allowed. In addition, he just threw himself into everything that had to do with his vocation as a Jesuit. It was as if he had been born for this time.

It's so hard to share the power of this Saint, who only lived a short time. We know so much about him, and yet we know nothing. He accomplished everything the Lord wanted of him in his short life on earth, and yet there was so much more he wanted to be for Jesus, His Mother Mary, and his Heavenly Family of Angels and Saints. According to his Novice-master, Fr. Fazio, the little Saint went out of his way to make holy everything he did or said, from his prayer life to working in the kitchen "*finding God among the pots and pans.*"[8] He overstated his shortcomings to a great degree. His bodily disciplines were not regulated unless he went overboard, which he had a tendency to do. At such times, he was only kept in check for health purposes. In the beginning, his superiors felt he was too good to be true; but seeing his day in, and day out piety, they came to know him, and to realize he was real! Although he challenged his brother novices to be more, they did not resent him; rather they felt they

---

[8]Teresa of Avila - Bob & Penny Lord's book *"Saints and Other Powerful Women in the Church"*

were in the presence of a Saint, which indeed they were.

But when it was time for him to go, he knew, as Mary of Bethany, who *"has chosen the better portion, which shall not be taken away from her."*[9] that he was choosing the better portion.

Around the feast of Our Lady of the Snows (August 5) Stanislaus had a premonition that he was going to die. Now this did not come completely out of the blue. He had a difficult summer in Rome. It was sweltering, and he was not physically up to it. So while his statement about dying may have been considered somewhat rash, it was accepted that he was very sick. He made a statement to one of the priests at St. Andrew's. He said, *"How happy a day for all the Saints was that on which the Blessed Virgin was received into Heaven! Perhaps the blessed celebrate it with special joy, as we do on earth. I hope myself to be there for the next feast they will keep of it."*[10]

A few days later, he was given a room with more ventilation in the hopes of reviving his respiratory system. His novice master tried to treat lightly his statement about dying. He said to him, "Oh man of little heart, do you give up for so slight a thing?" to which our little Saint replied, *"I am a man of little heart, but it is not so slight a matter, for I shall die of it."*[11] It was at this point that the Jesuits in the residence remembered Stanislaus' statement before he was afflicted with the illness which finally became his last; as he had prophesied. He actually predicted to a brother who was taking care of him that he would die the *following day,* but the brother ignored his statement. That night he was anointed and signed by his brothers (with the Sign of the Cross). He was given Viaticum;[12] his face changed from a painful grimace into a sweet, peaceful smile. He asked to be placed on the floor, rather than the bed. He was heard to pray

---

[9]Luke 10:42

[10]Butler's Lives of the Saints Vol IV - Pg 336

[11]Butler's Lives of the Saints Vol IV - Pg 336

[12]Last Communion, as part of the Last Rites of the Church. Today it would be part of the Anointing of the Sick

softly, *"My heart is ready, O God, my heart is ready!"* He went into a peaceful sleep.

But he knew that of which he spoke. He prophesied that he would die on the 15th, and he was not about to back down from his promise. Early on the morning of the Feast of Our Lady's Assumption into Heaven, August 15, our little Saint breathed his last. He whispered to Fr. Ruiz that he had seen Our Lady coming for him with many Angels. His face was radiant. They had never seen such a light coming from a human being. His Lady had come for her child; and she brought his Cousins - the Angels, and his Brothers and Sisters - the Saints, to welcome him into Heaven.

We would like to point out something at this juncture. Stanislaus always made mention of his Heavenly Family. He considered St. Barbara a very special, personal member of his Family. He had an intimate relationship with the Angels. Mother Mary came to him more than once. His biography mentions two times she visited him, including the time she came with the Angels and brought him into the Kingdom.

We believe we have a Heavenly Family. We believe the Saints are our Brothers and Sisters and the Angels are our Heavenly Cousins. Now, we have never personally seen Our Lady, nor have we had an intimate experience with the Angels, and yet we know that She protects us from all evil, and that the Angels, our Cousins, have been with us since before we were born, and will remain with us until we die. Then when we leave Purgatory, we believe Our Lady and the Angels will come to take us *Home* to Heaven. The Angels will be led by St. Michael, Prince of the Heavenly Hosts, and we will make a glorious entry into the Kingdom, where all our Brothers and Sisters - the Saints, will be there to welcome us. Jesus, the Holy Spirit and God the Father will welcome us, as well. St. Stanislaus believed this. He lived to experience it and tell us about it. Praise God!

Brother Paul turned up like a bad penny, the month after Stanislaus died. He had been dispatched by his father from

Poland to bring Stanislaus back, no matter the cost. Probably Paul had many distractions along the way, parties of one kind or another, lady friends who delayed him from keeping his appointment to take his brother home. But he was shocked, into sobriety possibly, when he learned of his brother's death. Stanislaus' death had a profound effect on brother Paul. Sadly, his life did not have the effect, but his death. At any rate, Paul re-evaluated his attitude and conduct towards his brother. Dr. Bilinsky also berated Paul on the way he mistreated St. Stanislaus. The two were used as witnesses to a great degree by the investigators after the Cause for St. Stanislaus' Canonization was opened. Dr. Bilinsky criticized Paul soundly. He stated as a witness, *"The blessed boy (Stanislaus) never had a good word from Paul. And we both knew all the time the holiness and devotion of all that he did."*[13] This also gave Paul cause to consider how badly he had treated his brother.

A conversion came about with regard to Paul. He blamed himself to a degree for the death of his younger brother. He was repentant for the rest of his life. A good thing happened, however. At age sixty, he asked to be admitted into the Society of Jesus.

Stanislaus was the *first* member of the Society of Jesus to be beatified; and that it was bestowed on a novice who was only with the order for ten months, made it even more incredulous. It was in 1605, only thirty-six years after his death, Stanislaus was declared *Blessed Stanislaus*; to be later canonized on December 31, 1726.

He was made Patron Saint of the youth of Poland. When Saint *Stanislaus* Kostka was raised to the Communion of Saints, it was, as well, a great honor bestowed on the church of Poland and her people; but it was also a great challenge, not so much for what he did, because he didn't do anything monumental in the eyes of the world; he did not found an order, he didn't open

---

[13]Butler's Lives of the Saints Vol IV - Pg 336

schools, he didn't go to far-off places as a missionary; he didn't do much of anything, except live a life of holiness, which would earn him a crown in Heaven.

He traded in fame on earth, relinquishing his position in the nobility, with its worldly treasures, for everlasting peace and joy in the Kingdom of God. He has been given to us, to the Church, and to the world as a role model for what mankind can be, not necessarily what it is. He is not only for the young, he is for all ages and all times, but especially for these days, where we are embarking on a new millennium, a new opportunity to be holy.

I am placing my bets on the young - that they will change the world - because I have seen young people striving to be holy, to be Saints, other Stanislauses and Maria Gorettis, other Dominic Savios and Roses of Viterbo, Aloysius Gonzagas and Margarets of Castello, Gabriel Possentis and Philomenas, to mention just a few Saints who challenge us to be more.

This Saint is a Role Model for the young and those who strive for holiness, and Sainthood. Strive to be Saints! The Lord honored Aloysius for his ability to *be*, not his ability to *do*. Follow in his footsteps. Love Jesus and Mary. Stay in touch with your Heavenly Family.

Epilog

Family, our children are not only the future of our Church, they are the future of our world. It is crystal clear why the *enemy* has been attacking our younger generation with a passion these last fifty years. In the 1960's, the Satan of drugs killed more young people each year than died in the *entire* Vietnam War! And those who didn't die, became the mindless dead walking in a daze, feeling nothing, caring little, a lost generation. They were our future Presidents of the United States, our congressmen and senators, governors, mayors, future priests, religious sisters and brothers, scientists, doctors, lawyers, fathers and mothers of future generations. *And we did nothing!*

And when that did not bring about the long-range plans of total domination and annihilation of our country and the world fast enough, the enemy of God began to poison our children's minds with not only mind-altering drugs, but mind-altering music, encouraging all kinds of death and sin leading to not only demise of the body, but of the soul. *And we did nothing!*

Sex education and encouraged permissiveness resulted with children in many states (without having to get parents' permission) endangering their lives, dying on the abortionist's table along with their unborn babies; deluded feminists calling it free choice. Catholic countries voted in first divorce and then abortion; the foolish being sold a bill of goods - falling for the devil's own propaganda machine that we can go to Heaven without dying; we can have Easter Sunday without the Cross. No suffering; no inconvenience, no pain, no gain!

And soon, we cry out, *Where have the children gone?* They have robbed our children of their innocent years, little girls wearing makeup by ten and some experimenting in things no one of any age should engage in. *Oh, where have the children gone?* The enemy and his cohorts have come in the dead of night and stolen our children's innocence. I look at movies of the 1940's and 50's and I cry out, *What have you done with my world?*

The enemy has tried many ploys to destroy the people of God. His most effective weapon has been fired at us like an invisible gas. You don't see it; you don't smell it; and at first, you don't feel it. But it creeps up on you and eventually strangles you as it is strangling our society today. That weapon is *Apathy*. We don't care. That's just the way the powers of hell want you to react. But that's the biggest mistake we can make. *Our children have no one on their side if they don't have us.*

One major reason Pope John Paul II has such a great rapport with the youth, why they come out by the millions to be in the presence of this man who is approaching eighty years old, is that he treats them like he would treat an adult, with respect and dignity and love. He sees in them what we have to see in them, the future of our world. He sees hope in them, the hope of a new culture, a culture of life to combat the culture of death which we have not defeated because of mass Apathy. You can reach your children; they're not lost to you or your family. Do what the Pope does; reach out to them with love.

We are alive, brothers and sisters. *We have not yet begun to fight!* But we will; we must! *We love our Church!* And although there are problems, she is the best there is, and *we love our country!* We love our hymns and Sunday Mass. We love our flag and we still cry when we sing the National Anthem and say the Pledge of Allegiance. We are Catholics first and Americans second, but Americans none-the-less. This is our Church and our country. And while we have a breath of life left in our bodies, we are going to fight for our children, of every color, creed and race; for they are all ours, children loaned to us by God Our Father. We are going to fight, so that they have a Church to go to and a country to live in where they can worship without fear!

We love you, family! Love your children. Save the world.

Bibliography

Fr. Camillus, C.P - *Saint Gabriel, Passionist*
    Catholic Publishing, New York 1953
Mead, Jude C.P.   *St. Gabriel, Passionist*
    L'Eco di San Gabriele, Teramo Italy 1985
Farnum, Mabel - *Saint Gabriel*
    Society of St. Paul Canfield, Ohio 1950
Tylenda, Joseph N. SJ - *Jesuit Saints & Martyrs*
    Loyola University Press - Chicago, IL 1983
Butler, Thurston & Atwater - *Lives of the Saints*
    Christian Classics, Westminster, Maryland 1980
Simoni, Rino - *Luoghi Aloisiani*
    Santuario di San L. Gonzaga - Castiglione D.S. Italy 1991
O'Sullivan, Fr. Paul O.P. - *Saint Philomena, Wonder Worker*
    Tan Publications - Rockford, IL 1993
Mohr, Sr. Marie Helene S.C. - Saint Philomena
    Tan Publications - Rockford, IL 1988
Poage, Godfrey C.P. - *In Garments all Red*
    Ave Maria Institute Washington NJ 1972
Alberti, Giovanni Fr. C.P. - *Marietta*, Story of Maria Goretti
    Sanctuary of Maria Goretti, Nettuno Italy 1980
Bosco, St. John - *St. Dominic Savio*
    Don Bosco Publications, New Rochelle, NY 1955
Piacentini, Ernesto-*Il Libro dei Miracoli di Sta. Rosa da Viterbo*
    Basilica di S. Francesco alla Rocca - Viterbo, Italy 1991
Cenci, Paolo - *Breve Narrazione della Vita di Santa Rosa*
    Monastero di Santa Rosa in Viterbo Italy 1971
Valentini Ubaldo - *Beata Margherita de la Metola*
    Instituto Beata Margherita, Città di Castello Italy 1988
Bonniwell Wm. O.P. - *Blessed Margaret of Castello*
    Tan Publications, Rockford, IL 1983
Lord, Bob & Penny - *Saints & Other Powerful Women in the Church*
Journeys of Faith, Westlake Village, CA 1989

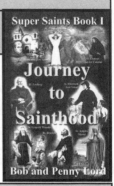

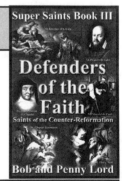

Videos available based on this book

St. Maria Goretti

Bob& Penny Lord

V147 - Saint Maria Goretti
Go to **Corinaldo, Italy,** where St. Maria Goretti was born and lived her early years, and on to **Nettuno, Italy,** where she died defending her virginity. See the **room in which she lived.**

St. Aloysius Gongaga

Bob& Penny Lord

V154 - St. Aloysius Gonzaga
From riches to rags, he answered the call to evangelize, going from Spain to Florence to Mantua where he served in the king's court to Casale Monferrato in northern Italy to the Gesu.

St. Dominic Savio

Bob& Penny Lord

V156 - Saint Dominic Savio
Come to Turin, Italy, to Don Bosco's Oratory where his most famous student, Dominic Savio, shone. Learn how he stood up for purity against all odds. See his home town in Castelnuovo.

Bl. Margaret of Castello

Bob& Penny Lord

V157 - Bl. Margaret of Castello
Known as the Saint of Pro-life, Margaret was not wanted and abandoned by her parents because of her deformity. Come to Cittá di Castello where her body lies incorrupt in her church.

St. Rose of Viterbo

Bob& Penny Lord

V159 - Saint Rose of Viterbo
A fiery teen-age Saint who fought almost single-handedly against family, friends and the government to defend the Church against Frederick Barbarossa in her little village outside of Rome.

St. Philomena

Bob& Penny Lord

V160 - Saint Philomena
One of the most popular Saints. We go from Rome where her relics were unearthed to her shrine in Mugnano, Italy, near Naples. Learn about the miracles attributed to her.

St. Stanilaus Kostka

Bob& Penny Lord

V163 - Saint Stanilaus Kostka
Venerated as the patron of youth because he died at 17. Also, secondary patron Saint of Poland. He devoted himself to God and the Society of Jesus. He joined the Jesuits and was a model novitiate.

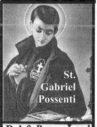

V164 - Saint Gabriel Possenti
Born in Assisi, he moved to Spoleto before a great Cholera epidemic broke out. Visit Morrovalle, where he spent most of his life as a brother, and then to Isola di Gran Sasso, where he died.

Produced by Journeys of Faith®
To Order call 1-800-633-2484

Journeys of Faith®

Books

Bob and Penny Lord are authors of best sellers:

This Is My Body, This Is My Blood;
Miracles of the Eucharist Book I $9.95 Paperback
This Is My Body, This Is My Blood;
Miracles of the Eucharist Book II $13.95 Paperback
The Many Faces Of Mary, A Love Story $9.95 Paperback $13.95 Hardcover
We Came Back To Jesus $9.95 Paperback $13.95 Hardcover
Saints and Other Powerful Women in the Church $13.95 Paperback
Saints and Other Powerful Men in the Church $14.95 Paperback
Heavenly Army of Angels $13.95 Paperback
Scandal of the Cross and Its Triumph $13.95 Paperback
The Rosary - The Life of Jesus and Mary $13.95 Hardcover
Martyrs - They Died for Christ $13.95 Paperback
Visionaries, Mystics, and Stigmatists $13.95 Paperback
Visions of Heaven, Hell and Purgatory $13.95 Paperback
Treasures of the Church - That which makes us Catholic $9.95 Paperback
Tragedy of the Reformation $9.95 Paperback
Cults - Battle of the Angels $9.95 Paperback
Trilogy (3 Books - Treasure..., Tragedy... and Cults...) $25.00 Paperback
Journey to Sainthood - Founders, Confessors & Visionaries $10.95 Paperback
Holy Innocence - The Young and the Saintly $10.95 Paperback
Defenders of the Faith - Saints of the Counter-Reformation $10.95 Paperback
Super Saints Trilogy (3 Books - Journey ... Holy... Defenders...) $25.00

Please add $4.00 S&H for first book: $1.00 each add'l book

Videos and On-site Documentaries

Bob and Penny's Video Series based on their books:
13 part series on the Miracles of the Eucharist - 15 part series on The Many Faces of Mary - 23 part series on Martyrs - They Died for Christ - 10 part series on Visionaries, Mystics and Stigmatists - 50 part series on the Super Saints Trilogy
Many other on-site Documentaries based on Miracles of the Eucharist, Mother Mary's Apparitions, and the Heavenly Army of Angels. Request our list.
Our books and videos are available in Spanish also

Pilgrimages

Bob and Penny Lord's ministry take out Pilgrimages to the Shrines of Europe, and Mexico every year. Come and join them on one of these special Retreat Pilgrimages. Call for more information, and ask for the latest pilgrimage brochure.

Lecture Series

Bob and Penny travel to all parts of the world to spread the Good News. They speak on what they have written about in their books. If you would like to have them come to your area, call for information on a lecture series in your area.

Good Newsletter

We are publishers of the Good Newsletter, which is published four times a year. This newsletter will provide timely articles on our Faith, plus keep you informed with the activities of our community. Call 1-800-633-2484 for information.